Preparing Parish Liturgies

Preparing Parish Liturgies

A Guide to Resources

⌘

RITA THIRON

LITURGICAL PRESS
Collegeville, Minnesota

www.litpress.org

2	3	4	5	6	7	8

Library of Congress Cataloging-in-Publication Data

Thiron, Rita.
    Preparing parish liturgies : a guide to resources / Rita Thiron. — 1st ed.
      p. cm.
    Includes bibliographical references and index.
    ISBN 0-8146-2980-6 (alk. paper)
    1. Liturgics.   I. Title.
    BV178.T45 2004
    264'.02—dc22

                                                2003025465

Dedicated
to my family
whose love and support
make ministry possible

Contents

Abbreviations

Liturgical Books and Their *Praenotanda*

BB	Book of Blessings (1989)
BG	Book of the Gospels (2000)
CB	Ceremonial of Bishops (1989)
GILH	General Instruction on the Liturgy of the Hours (1971)
GIRM	General Instruction of the Roman Missal, *Institutio Generalis Missalis Romani* (2002)
GNLYC	General Norms for the Liturgical Year and the Calendar (1969)
HCWEOM	Holy Communion and Worship of the Eucharist outside of Mass (1973)
IBG	Introduction to the Book of the Gospels (2000)
LM	*Lectionary for Mass* (1969, 1981)
LMI	Lectionary for Mass: An Introduction (1998)
OCF	Order of Christian Funerals (1989)
OSEHE	Order of Solemn Exposition of the Holy Eucharist (1992)
PCS	Pastoral Care of the Sick (1982)
RBC	Rite of Baptism for Children (1969)
RCIA	Rite of Christian Initiation of Adults (1987)
RDCA	Rite of Dedication of a Church and an Altar (1989)
RM	Roman Missal (*Missale Romanum*) third typical edition (2002)
RP	Roman Pontifical (1972–1979)

The Constitution and Instructions on It

SC	*Sacrosanctum Concilium*: Constitution on the Sacred Liturgy (12-4-63)
IO	*Inter Oecumenici*: Principles for Carrying Out the Liturgical Renewal (9-26-64)

IRL   Inculturation and the Roman Liturgy: Fourth Instruction for the Right Application of the Conciliar Constitution on the Liturgy, nos. 37–40 (1-25-94)

LA   *Liturgiam Authenticam*: Fifth Instruction for the Right Application of the Conciliar Constitution on the Liturgy (3-28-01)

LI   *Liturgicae Instraurationes*: Central Role of the Bishop in the Renewal of the Liturgy (9-5-70)

TAA   *Tres Abhinc Annos*: Adaptations to the Order of Mass (5-4-67)

Documents

BBGI   Book of Blessings: General Introduction (1989)

BLS   Built of Living Stones (2000)

CEIL   Criteria for the Evaluation of Inclusive Language Translations of Scriptural Texts Proposed for Liturgical Use (1990)

CP   *Comme le Prévoit*: On the Translation of Liturgical Texts for Celebrations with a Congregation (1969)

DD   *Dies Domini*: On Keeping the Lord's Day Holy (1998)

DAPNE   Directory for the Application of Principles and Norms of Ecumenism (1993)

DMC   Directory for Masses with Children (1973)

DSCAP   Directory for Sunday Celebrations in the Absence of a Priest (1988)

EE   *Ecclesia de Eucharistia* (2003)

FYH   Fulfilled in Your Hearing: The Homily in the Sunday Assembly (1982)

GFT   Gather Faithfully Together (1997)

GSPD   Guidelines for the Celebration of the Sacraments with Persons with Disabilities (1995)

GMEF   God's Mercy Endures Forever: Guidelines on the Presentation of Jews and Judaism in Catholic Preaching (1988)

IOM:PR   Introduction to the Order of Mass: A Pastoral Resource of the BCL (2003)

LMT   Liturgical Music Today (1982)

MCW   Music in Catholic Worship (1972)

NDRHC   Norms for the Distribution and Reception of Holy Communion Under Both Kinds in the Dioceses of the United States of America (2002)

PGR   Plenty Good Room: The Spirit and Truth of African American Catholic Worship (1990)

PS   *Paschale Solemnitatis*: Circular Letter on Preparing and Celebrating the Paschal Feasts (1988)

RDCA   Rite of Dedication of a Church and an Altar (1989)

TSCC   To Speak as a Christian Community: Pastoral Message on Inclusive
        Language (1989)

Other

BCL   Bishops' Committee on the Liturgy

BVM   Blessed Virgin Mary

CCC   Catechism of the Catholic Church

CDW   Congregation for Divine Worship

CDWDS   Congregation for Divine Worship and the Discipline of the Sacraments

ICEL   The International Committee on English in the Liturgy

NCCB   National Conference of Catholic Bishops

SCDW   Sacred Congregation for Divine Worship

USCCB   United States Conference of Catholic Bishops

Chapter I

Principles of
Liturgical Preparation

The Sacred Triduum is several months away. The parish celebration of First Communion will follow soon afterward, and you're still trying to write a Lenten penance service. Has anyone talked to Father about the readings or can you just pick some from the Bible? Have the palms arrived? Should we order a taller paschal candle this year? Can we choose another reading for next Monday's Mass? Are there special prayers for that feast? Should we sing the same songs we have sung for the past two years and, if not, will the choir and assembly have enough rehearsal time? Who will train the greeters? What's a liturgist to do?

Relax. This book comes to assist parish staffs and worship commission members who are charged with the task of preparing and evaluating meaningful parish liturgies. It will acquaint you with the liturgical books, documents, and other resources with which you will want to be familiar. Before you open those resources, though, you should have an understanding of the task at hand. Let's begin with basic principles for liturgical preparation.

A DEFINITION OF LITURGY

First, it would help to define what liturgy is so that we might establish and focus on a set of goals. Liturgy is the official, communal worship of the Church. The term comes from the Greek *leitourgia* which means "the work of the people." In fact, that might be translated into even stronger language— "the public work of the people done on behalf of the people." The work is actually God's work and we are invited to participate in it (CCC 1069). This work (of God and ours) accomplishes a purpose and derives some benefit—"God's glorification and human sanctification" (SC 10).

Liturgy, by its very nature, is communal. The assembly is not a collection of people praying singularly in the same place, but a community of people that, by joining in this common prayer, manifest who and whose they are.

Moreover, our parish assemblies must remember that they are merely a part of a greater whole. In communion with other assemblies around the world and with the heavenly hosts, the Church visible and invisible, we offer due praise to God. "The liturgy is thus the outstanding means by which the faithful can express in their lives and manifest to others the mystery of Christ and the real nature of the true Church" (SC 2).

> [T]he liturgy is the summit toward which the activity of the Church is directed. At the same time, it is the fount from which all her power flows. The aim and object of apostolic works is that all who are made children of God by faith and baptism should come together to praise God in the midst of his Church, to take part in the sacrifice, and to eat the Lord's Supper. . . . From the liturgy, there-

fore, particularly from the Eucharist, grace is poured forth upon us as from a fountain; the liturgy is the source for achieving in the most effective way possible human sanctification and God's glorification, the end to which all the Church's other activities are directed (SC 10).

Liturgy, then, is not about what St. John's parish "does" on Sunday morning at 10:00. It is about what God accomplishes in all of us in communion with each of us.

In light of that, this author offers ten basic principles of liturgical preparation. You and your parish worship commission might develop more.

TEN BASIC PRINCIPLES OF LITURGICAL PREPARATION

(1) It's all about the paschal mystery!

I often get calls at the Office of Worship for evaluation tools. The caller invariably asks, "How can we judge whether we are doing liturgy correctly?" While many approaches could be taken, a simple five-word question will suffice: "Was the paschal mystery celebrated?"

Through Jesus' passion, death, resurrection, and glorious ascension, our redemption has been accomplished.

[W]hen the fullness of time had come, [God] sent his Son, the Word made flesh, anointed by the Holy Spirit, to preach the gospel to the poor, to heal the contrite of heart; he is the physician, being both flesh and of the Spirit, the mediator between God and us. For his humanity, united with the person of the Word, was the instrument of our salvation. Therefore in Christ, the perfect achievement of our reconciliation came forth and the fullness of divine worship was given to us. . . . He achieved his task of redeeming humanity and giving perfect glory to God, principally by the paschal mystery of his blessed passion, resurrection from the dead, and glorious ascension, whereby "dying he destroyed our death and rising he restored our life." For it was from the side of Christ as he slept the sleep of death upon the cross that there came forth the sublime sacrament of the whole Church (SC 5).

We celebrate what God has already accomplished in Christ *and our participation in it!* We recognize that our redemption has occurred, that God is with us now in his sacraments and his Church, yet we anticipate what is to come. This tension of "the already and the not-yet" is evident in our prayers; note the past, present, and future tense of the verbs. We recount what God has done, acknowledge his role in our lives now, and long for the day when we can see him face to face in the fullness of the kingdom. "When we eat this bread and drink this cup we proclaim your death, Lord Jesus, until you come in glory" (Memorial Acclamation; cf. 1 Cor 11:26).

Liturgy, then, should change us. It should bring about our conversion. The Word of God that challenges us, the sacraments that nourish us, and the assembly with which we pray all work to bring us closer to a share of Christ's divine nature.

(2) Every liturgy is the function of the priestly office of Jesus Christ.

This work of our redemption is ongoing and Christ continues to be present among us. Echoing earlier documents, the Constitution on the Sacred Liturgy (7) reminds us that Christ is present at every liturgical celebration in four ways—in the minister, in the Word, in the eucharistic species, and in the members of the assembly.

> To accomplish so great a work, Christ is always present in his Church, especially in its liturgical celebrations. He is present in the sacrifice of the Mass, not only in the person of his minister, "the same now offering, through the ministry of priests, who formerly now offered himself on the cross," but especially under the eucharistic elements. By his power He is present in the sacraments, so that when a man baptizes it is really Christ himself who baptizes. He is present in his word, since it is he himself who speaks when the holy Scriptures are read in the Church. He is present, lastly, when the Church prays and sings, for he promised: "Where two or three are gathered together in my name, there am I in the midst of them"(Mt 18:20).
>
> Christ always truly associates the Church with himself in this great work wherein God is perfectly glorified and the recipients made holy. The Church is the Lord's beloved Bride who calls to him and through him offers worship to the eternal Father.
>
> Rightly, then, the liturgy is considered as an exercise of the priestly office of Jesus Christ. In the liturgy, by means of signs perceptible to the senses, human sanctification is signified and brought about in ways proper to each of these signs; in the liturgy, the whole public worship is performed by the Mystical Body of Jesus Christ, that is, by the Head and his members.
>
> From this it follows that every liturgical celebration, because it is an action of Christ the Priest and of his Body which is the Church, is a sacred action surpassing all others. No other action of the Church can equal its effectiveness by the same title and to the same degree (SC 7).

Who gathers us together? God himself invites us. Through Jesus Christ and in the grace of the Holy Spirit we, the Body of Christ, encounter the living God.

(3) Recognize the role of the assembly.

If every liturgical celebration is "an action of Christ the priest and of his Body the Church" (SC 7), it follows that the role of the entire liturgical assembly is extremely important.

In the reform and promotion of the liturgy, this full and active participation by all the people is the aim to be considered before all else. For it is the primary and indispensable source from which the faithful are to derive the true Christian spirit and therefore pastors must zealously strive in all their pastoral work to achieve such participation by means of the necessary instruction (SC 14).

First, the liturgical formation of the assembly is essential to the vitality of the parish. Do the parishioners have an appreciation of the paschal mystery? Do they understand that the liturgical year unfolds various facets of that mystery? Do they understand the structure of the Mass?

Pastors must therefore realize that when the liturgy is celebrated something more is required than the mere observance of the laws governing valid and lawful celebration; it is also their duty to ensure that the faithful take part more fully aware of what they are doing, actively engaged in the rite, and enriched by its effects (SC 11).

The reformed liturgy presupposes a variety of competent ministers, each at the service of the assembly, well trained and faithful to their calling.

In liturgical celebrations, each one, minister or layperson, who has an office to perform, should do all of, but only, those parts which pertain to that office by the nature of the rite and the principles of liturgy (SC 28).

Servers, readers, commentators, and members of the choir also exercise a genuine liturgical function. They ought to discharge their office, therefore, with the sincere devotion and decorum demanded by so exalted a ministry and rightly expected of them by God's people. Consequently they must all be deeply imbued with the spirit of the Liturgy, in the measure proper to each one, and they must be trained to perform their functions in a correct and orderly manner (SC 29; cf. GIRM 91).

Liturgy is neither a show to be watched nor a play to be appreciated by an audience. Preparation, then, should never take on an "us *vs.* them" mentality, nor concentrate on the role of the presider or ministers alone. Rather, preparation should begin with an appreciation of what the entire Church will accomplish and then examine each person's role in that important work (cf. SC 14, 26–32, 41–46; GIRM 91–111).

This demands that those who prepare the liturgy have made appropriate adaptations to the liturgy in light of the ages, language, culture, and education of the assembly. It assumes that the worship space is accessible to all persons, including the sanctuary, so that persons with disabilities may also exercise their ministry to God's people.

And just as the texts for the presider and other ministers are essential, all the members of the assembly may need worship aids to assist them in singing or otherwise responding during an unfamiliar rite. These need not include the entire text of a reading or presidential prayers.

(4) *Lex orandi, lex credendi.*

In the fifth century, Prosper of Aquitaine, a disciple of Augustine, was arguing against semi-Pelagianism. The debate centered around the issue of the necessity of grace to even come to faith. Did God initiate our faith life or could we do that without him? To answer that, Prosper turned to the liturgy.

We must be dependent on God, he reasoned, because every day, we petition him for his help. The proof was in our prayer life! "*Ut legem credendi, lex statuat supplicandi,*" he asserted. Specifically, the intercessions *petition God* for every human need; therefore, we must be dependent on him. Countless leaders and theologians since have come to the same conclusion as Prosper—prayer and doctrine are mutually confirming.

The shortened axiom, *lex orandi, lex credendi*, simply put, means that the rules of our prayer are the rules of our belief. That is, the words of our prayer reflect what we believe; they are consistent with our doctrine. Likewise, our doctrine reflects long-held patterns of the Church at prayer. The Church has used this argument time and again. In 1950, when Pope Pius XII proclaimed the dogma of the Assumption, he used the argument that the Church, under the guidance of the Holy Spirit, had celebrated Mary's Assumption [Dormition] since the fourth century.

The Church takes very seriously the composition and translation of our liturgical prayer, making certain that it mirrors the precepts of our faith. So in preparing parish liturgy, we stick to the script, so to speak. Carefully using the liturgical books and their official translations, we routinely express and foster our faith. We can confidently turn to the Church's liturgy for catechesis and find in its readings, rituals, and prayer texts a treasury of doctrine and tradition.

(5) Always begin with the rite.

Whether we are preparing a communal penance service, a wedding, a funeral, or weekday Mass, the first step must be to look at the rite. That's why this book is very purposefully titled *Preparing Parish Liturgies: A Guide to the Church's Resources.* Liturgies are not *planned*, they are *prepared*. The Church has already "planned" them; we simply prepare our assemblies and those who minister to them to celebrate what the Church has already built from centuries of doctrine and praxis.

It is important to use the current edition of the rite. Check the front of the book for a date or the promulgation decree. The Pope, Vatican office, or conference of bishops who promulgated the decree will usually include a sentence such as "all things to the contrary notwithstanding." This makes other editions invalid. You may also see a sentence such as "published for use in the dioceses of the United States" which declares that this edition or translation of the rite was developed for the USA and will be the only one used in the dioceses of the USA. In some cases, the text will include various adaptations to the *editio typica* (typical edition) that have been approved by the USCCB for use in the USA.

The *praenotanda*, or the introductory notes, are important. They always begin with a theology of the sacrament or rite, then elaborate on what God and his people are about to accomplish. They may also include details on the proper or usual times (the day[s] this rite can and cannot be celebrated); the proper place for its celebration; the usual minister of the rite; his/her vesture; the structure of the rite; and any adaptations that might be made to it.

Christian Initiation: General Introduction is a fine example of such introductory remarks:

> Baptism incorporates us into Christ and forms us into God's people. This first sacrament pardons all our sins, rescues us from the power of darkness, and brings us to the dignity of adopted children, a new creation through water and the Holy Spirit. Hence, we are called and are indeed children of God.
>
> By signing us with the gift of the Spirit, confirmation makes us more completely the image of the Lord and fills us with the Holy Spirit, so that we may bear witness to him before all the world and work to bring the Body of Christ to its fullness as soon as possible.
>
> Finally, coming to the table of the eucharist, we eat the flesh and drink the blood of the Son of Man so that we might have eternal life and show forth the unity of God's people. . . .
>
> Thus the three sacraments of Christian initiation closely combine to bring us, the faithful of Christ, to his full stature and to enable us to carry out the mission of the entire people of God in the Church and in the world (CIGI 2).

Besides theological principles, the *praenotanda* may include juridic norms. These tell us what is to be done in the rite and how to do it. Some contain words such as "must," "must not," "is to" or are written in the third person ("the priest genuflects"). These prescribe an action that must take place. Other norms include words such as "should," "may," or "is proper," and these mild commands describe what is generally or ideally done. Still other norms alert the presider or other persons to options—other texts, readings, or acclamations. "In these or similar words" and "sings or says" are frequently printed within the rites. A word of caution about this last type—you must choose from among the options.

Thus, the rite itself, especially in its *praenotanda,* instructs us as to its proper celebration. Likewise, the rite itself is the best tool for evaluating our celebrations—have we been faithful both to the theological principles and the juridic norms? Have we understood both the spirit and letter of the law?

(6) The Word is essential.

The bishops of Vatican II commanded that the "treasures of the Bible are to be opened up more lavishly, so that a richer sharing of God's word may be provided to the faithful . . . " (SC 51). All the revised rites include one or more readings from Sacred Scripture. They often supply a generous collection of optional readings in their appendices.

> When God shares his word with us, he awaits our response, that is, our listening and our adoring "in Spirit and in truth" (John 4:23). The Holy Spirit makes our response effective, so that what we hear in the celebrations of the liturgy, we carry out in the way we live: "Be doers of the word and not hearers only" (James 1:22).
>
> The liturgical celebration and the faithful's participation receive outward expressions in actions, gestures, and words. These derive their full meaning not simply from their origin in human experience but from the word of God and the economy of salvation, their point of reference. Accordingly, the faithful's participation in the liturgy increases to the degree that as they listen to the word of God spoken in the liturgy they strive harder to commit themselves to the Word of God made flesh in Christ. They endeavor to conform their way of life to what they celebrate in the liturgy, and then in turn bring to the celebration of the liturgy all that they do in life (*Introduction, Lectionary for Mass,* no. 6).

(7) Allow the ritual to speak.

The Roman Rite is, and nearly always has been, composed using the principle of "noble simplicity," i.e., it uses simple, well-selected words and brief sentences.

> The rites should be marked by noble simplicity; they should be short, clear, and unencumbered by useless repetitions; they should be within the people's power of comprehension and as a rule not require much explanation (SC 34).

Besides words, our rites also rely on symbols and signs, gestures, and postures to convey deeper meanings.

A ritual is a repeated, familiar pattern of behavior that conveys meaning and often offers the participant a sense of identity. For example, even when you attend Mass in another town, you recognize that you are participating in a Catholic liturgy because the ritual pattern is familiar to you.

The profession of faith, pouring of water, anointing with oil, and clothing with a white garment conjure up in our minds far greater understanding of what is taking place—initiation into the life and death of Jesus Christ. Even our gestures, such as a sign of the cross, remind us who and whose we are.

A symbol, by its very nature, is multivalent. For example, water gives life, cleanses, recalls creation, etc. The Church has always used "signs perceptible to the senses" (SC 7) to convey the living presence of God among us. Sacramental signs effect what they symbolize; e.g., the waters of baptism cleanse us from our sins. Symbols engage the assembly and its ministers in the deeds that define them (*Gather Faithfully Together,* 141).

A stop sign does not require a verbal warning to stop, nor does a wedding ring on the third finger of a left hand necessitate a written explanation of the married state to anyone who sees it. These signs, by themselves, indicate a clear meaning. Are your signs adequate? Are your symbols speaking? Are baptisms conducted over a bowl of water or are the Elect lavishly immersed in "enough water to drown in" since they are being baptized into the life and death of Jesus Christ? Is the Eucharist routinely distributed under both kinds—the Body and the Blood of Christ? Is the paschal candle, a sign of the light of Christ, short and narrow or tall, full, and tastefully decorated? Does the smoke of the incense fill the space or does it disappear almost immediately? Is your *Book of the Gospels* worthy of its contents?

(8) Environment affects worship.

The first generations of Christians celebrated liturgy in homes. When communities moved from house churches to basilicas or courthouses, they adopted the pomp and vesture of royalty and the court system. This, in turn, colored liturgical practices. Later, the installation of rood screens and the separation of the people from the altar impacted the very understanding of the Eucharist; it was no longer a meal to be shared but an object to be adored. The placement of pews and the elevation of the sanctuary spoke loudly of a hierarchical church structure, both architecturally and ecclesiastically.

When the Second Vatican Council called for the reform of the rites, it followed that our worship spaces must change with them, since "the full and active participation of the people [was] the aim to be considered above all else" (SC 14).

So those who prepare liturgy must also assess the space in which the liturgical action will take place. Where are the altar, ambo, and presider chair in proximity to the assembly? Is the furniture, especially the altar and ambo, well crafted from worthy materials? Does the entire space convey a sense of the sacred? Even when finances are tight and multiple activities happen in or nearby, do we treat the worship area with respect?

The church is the proper place for the liturgical prayer of the parish community, especially the celebration of the Eucharist on Sunday. It is also the privileged place for adoration of the Blessed Sacrament and reservation of the Eucharist for Communion for the sick. Whenever communities have built houses for worship, the design of the building has been of critical importance. Churches are never simply gathering spaces but signify and make visible the church living in [a particular] place, the "dwelling of God" among us, now "reconciled and united in Christ." As such the building itself becomes "a sign of the pilgrim Church on earth and reflects the Church dwelling in heaven." Every church building is a gathering place for the assembly, a resting place, a place of encounter with God, as well as a point of departure on the Church's unfinished journey toward the reign of God (BLS 17, cf. RDCA 1–2; CCC 1180, 2691).

Churches therefore, must be places "suited to sacred celebrations, dignified and beautiful. Their suitability for worship is determined by their ability through the architectural design of space and the application of artistic gifts to embody God's initiative and the community's faithful response. Church buildings and religious artworks that beautify them are forms of worship themselves and both inspire and reflect the prayer of the community as well as the inner life of grace. Conversely, church buildings and religious artifacts that are trivial, contrived, or lack beauty can detract from the church's liturgy. Architecture and art become the joint work of the Holy Spirit and the local community, that of preparing human hearts to receive God's word and to enter more fully into communion with God (BLS 18; cf. RDCA 2, *Letter to Artists* #12, 16; CCC 1098, BLS 50).

Practical matters are important, too. Have you ever tried to participate in a liturgy when a sound system was poor? You struggled to be attentive to God's word, but couldn't hear what the reader was saying. If the heating system was malfunctioning, your thoughts may have turned to feeling too cold. Parish worship commissions and ministers of hospitality must always be attentive to the assembly's basic comfort.

(9) Music is integral.

Music is not something we "add on" to a liturgical celebration. It is not optional. Indeed, it is vitally important to the celebration.

Among the many signs and symbols used by the church to celebrate its faith, music is of preeminent importance. As sacred song united to words, it forms a necessary or integral part of the solemn liturgy. Yet the function of music is ministerial; it must serve and never dominate. Music should assist the assembled believers to express and share the gift of faith that is within them and to nourish and strengthen their interior commitment of faith. It should heighten the texts so that they speak more fully and effectively. The quality of joy and enthusiasm which music adds to community worship cannot be gained in any other way. It imparts a sense of unity to the congregation and sets the appropriate tone for a particular celebration (MCW 23).

> The musical tradition of the universal Church is a treasure of inestimable value, greater even than that of any other art. The main reason for this preeminence is that, as sacred song closely bound to text, it forms a necessary or integral part of the solemn liturgy. Holy Scripture itself has bestowed praise upon sacred song and the same may be said of the fathers of the Church and the Roman Pontiffs who . . . have explained more precisely the ministerial function supplied by sacred music in the service of the Lord. Therefore sacred music will be the more holy the more closely it is joined to the liturgical rite, whether by adding more delight to prayer, fostering oneness of spirit, or investing the rites with greater solemnity . . . (SC 112).

> In addition to expressing texts, music can also unveil a dimension of meaning and feeling, a communication of ideas and intuitions which words alone cannot yield. This dimension is integral to the human personality and to growth in faith. It cannot be ignored if the signs of worship are to speak to the whole person. Ideally, every communal celebration of faith . . . should include music and singing . . . (MCW 24).

Music can accompany ritual action (e.g., chanting enough verses of the Lamb of God at the Breaking of the Bread). Music can also *be* the ritual action, when sung prayer is a constituent element of the rite itself, e.g., the *Gloria,* the Litany of the Saints in an initiation rite, or the solemn chanting of the Prayer of Ordination at an ordination rite (cf. *Liturgical Music Today,* 10).

> The first place to look for guidance in the use and choice of music is the rite itself. Often the rubrics contained in the approved liturgical books will indicate the place for song and will also prescribe or suggest an appropriate text to be set musically (LMT 8).

In addition to the careful selection of music, those who prepare and lead parish liturgies should make the hiring of competent music directors and the training of musicians, cantors, and choristers a priority in the parish's life and budget.

(10) Preparation and evaluation are imperative.

> The preparation of the liturgy is not the prerogative or the responsibility of the presider alone. On the contrary, the Church places great value in collaborative planning, not only for the liturgy itself, but also for the various parts of it, such as the homily (FYH 106–108).

> The pastoral effectiveness of a celebration will be greatly increased if the texts of the readings, the prayers, and the liturgical songs correspond as

closely as possible to the needs, spiritual preparation, and culture of those taking part. . . .

The priest, therefore, in planning the celebration of Mass, should have in mind the common spiritual good of the people of God, rather than his own inclinations. He should, moreover, remember that the selection of different parts is to be made in agreement with those who have some role in the celebration, including the faithful, in regard to the parts that more directly pertain to each.

Since, indeed, a variety of options is provided for the different parts of the Mass, it is necessary for the deacon, the lectors, the psalmist, the cantor, the commentator, and the choir to be completely sure before the celebration about those texts for which each is responsible is to be used and that nothing be improvised. Harmonious planning and carrying out of the rites will be of great assistance in disposing the faithful to take part in the Eucharist (GIRM 352; cf. GIRM chapters 7 and 8).

It would be especially effective to include not only a wide variety of ministers in a planning session, but also those with whom you will celebrate, e.g., the confirmation candidates, the godparents and sponsors, the bride and groom, and even the first communicants. When possible, grieving family members should be invited to participate in preparations for the funeral liturgy. This gives the parish ministers another opportunity to share the power of the funeral rites and to "bring hope and consolation to the living" (OCF 7).

A BRIEF WORD ABOUT PARISH WORSHIP COMMISSIONS

The Constitution on the Sacred Liturgy (44–46) saw the value in having a commission of experts in liturgy, music, and art to advise each diocesan bishop. Likewise, the parish worship commission serves as advisors to the pastor. With him, it (1) assesses the needs of the worshiping assembly, (2) supervises the training of competent liturgical ministers, (3) provides for the ongoing liturgical formation of the assembly, (4) develops parish policies for liturgical celebrations, (5) implements changes mandated by the diocesan bishop, and (6) routinely evaluates the liturgical celebrations of the parish.

Ideally, the commission is not charged with the actual preparation—they do not buy the red geraniums for Pentecost. Instead, they advise and guide those who do. In some parishes, this is accomplished by a subcommittee structure. For example, the coordinators of lectors, environment, and art, and extraordinary ministers of Holy Communion might sit on the commission and they, in turn, will see to it that the various directives of the pastor and commission are carried out.

The members of the parish worship commission should reflect the population of the parish assembly—young and old, male and female, racial considerations, etc. Moreover, each member must be committed to his or her own liturgical formation. Indeed, such formation should be a standing agenda item at each monthly meeting. The commission should subscribe to liturgical periodicals, read pertinent documents and books, and attend diocesan workshops and classes. Contact your diocesan worship office for assistance.

THE PURPOSE AND PREMISE OF THIS BOOK

This book will acquaint the reader with the liturgical books, related liturgical documents, and other resources for preparing the Church's liturgy.

In chapter II, the reader will explore the books that constitute the Roman Missal—the Sacramentary, Lectionary for Mass, the Book of the Gospels, and other related texts. In chapter III, the books that constitute the Roman Ritual and the Roman Pontifical will be delineated. The Liturgy of the Hours and Sunday Celebrations in the Absence of a Priest will be explored here, too. In chapters IV and V, one may examine significant liturgical documents. In treating these books and documents, I will provide a brief history and synopsis of the text and an outline of its contents. These outlines are the clearest and most succinct way for the reader to peruse the scope of the liturgical book or document, the logic of its sequence, and the full breadth of its options.

Armed with that background, the reader will then be invited to apply the information and wisdom from those texts to the privileged task of preparing a liturgy. Chapters VI to VIII will guide readers through the liturgical year, enabling them to make well-informed choices regarding a parish celebration.

It is my sincere hope that the reader may have a greater appreciation of the Church's liturgical history, tradition, and the liturgical renewal. Then, even novices can confidently prepare parish celebrations that are more faithful to the Church's liturgy and less exercises in creativity or frustration.

It is further hoped that, armed with accurate vocabulary and resources, all liturgical ministers, ordained and lay, can prepare more collaboratively. This will, in turn, foster the full, conscious, and active participation of the assembly—a participation "burning with faith, hope and charity, of the sort that is demanded by the very nature of the celebration, and to which the Christian people have a right and duty by reason of their baptism" (GIRM 18). All this will lead to the ultimate goal—the praise of almighty God and the sanctification of God's people.

FOR FURTHER READING

Black Catholic Liturgy Committee. *Plenty Good Room: The Spirit and Truth of African American Catholic Worship.* Washington, D.C.: USCCB, 1990.

Chapungo, Anscar J. *Liturgical Inculturation: Sacramentals, Religiosity, and Catechesis.* Collegeville: The Liturgical Press, 1992.

Francis, Mark R. *Guidelines for Multicultural Celebrations.* Washington, D.C.: Federation of Diocesan Liturgical Commissions, 1998.

Holland, Jim, ed. *Modern Liturgy Planning Guide.* San Jose: Resource Publications, Inc., 1987.

Hovda, Robert. *The Amen Corner.* John F. Baldovin, ed. Collegeville: The Liturgical Press/Pueblo Publishing Company, 1994.

Huck, Gabe. *The Three Days: Parish Prayer and the Paschal Triduum.* Archdiocese of Chicago: Liturgy Training Publications, 1992.

Huck, Gabe, and Gerald T. Chinchar. *Liturgy with Style and Grace* (third edition). Archdiocese of Chicago: Liturgy Training Publications, 1998.

Hynes, Mary Ellen. *Companion to the Calendar.* Archdiocese of Chicago: Liturgy Training Publications, 1993.

Johnson, Lawrence J. *The Three Days: A Liturgical Guide.* Washington, D.C.: Federation of Diocesan Liturgical Commissions, 2001.

Kavanaugh, Aidan. *On Liturgical Theology.* Collegeville: The Liturgical Press/Pueblo Publishing Company, 1984.

Kerwin, Patricia. "Minding Your P & Q's" *Liturgy 90* (May–June 1999) 1–9.

Gallen, John, Mary Alice Piil, et al. *Liturgy Plus* (computer software). San Francisco: Harper.

LabOra—a Liturgical Planning Aid on CD from the Liturgical Press.

Mazar, Peter. *To Crown the Year: Decorating the Church Through the Seasons.* Archdiocese of Chicago: Liturgy Training Publications, 1995.

Moroney, James P., ed. *Liturgy: Active Participation in the Divine Life, Where We've Been—Where We're Going.* Major Addresses from the 1989 National Meeting of the Diocesan Liturgical Commissions. Collegeville: The Liturgical Press, 1990.

Nuzzi, Ronald J. "Worship and People with Disabilities: Ten Tips," *Church Magazine.* New York: National Pastoral Life Center, 1999.

Ostdiek, Gilbert. *Catechesis for Liturgy.* Washington, D.C.: The Pastoral Press, 1986.

Perry, Bishop Joseph. "All You Nations Come! A Dialogue with Bishop Joseph Perry," *Liturgy 90* (April 1999). Archdiocese of Chicago: Liturgy Training Publications, 1999.

Richter, Klemens. *The Meaning of the Sacramental Symbols: Answers to Today's Questions.* Trans. Linda M. Maloney. Collegeville: The Liturgical Press, 1990.

St. Anthony Messenger Press, Cincinnati, Ohio. *Catholic Update.*
    Lent: A Forty-Day Retreat: Rediscovering Your Baptismal Call (February 1990)
    Lent: Balancing the Old and the New (February 1994)
    Lenten Stories from John's Gospel (March 1996)
    The Liturgical Year: How Christians Celebrate Time (November 1995)
    Our Holiest Week: A Practical Guide for Holy Week Liturgies (April 1992)
    Passover: Jewish Roots of the Eucharist (March 1998)
    A Step-by-Step Walk through the Mass (August 1989)
    Sunday Mass: Easter All Year Long (March 1999)

Searle, Mark. *Liturgy Made Simple.* Collegeville: The Liturgical Press, 1981.

————. *Of Piety and Planning: Liturgy, the Parishioners and the Professionals.* Notre Dame, Ind.: University of Notre Dame, 1985.

Smolarski, Dennis. *Liturgical Literacy: From Anamnesis to Worship.* New York: Paulist Press, 1990.

Sourcebook for Sundays and Seasons. Archdiocese of Chicago: Liturgy Training Publications, 2001.

USCCB. *Built of Living Stones.* Washington, D.C.: November 2000.

Vatican II. *Sacrosanctum Concilium,* Constitution on the Sacred Liturgy, December 4, 1963.

Wainwright, Geoffrey. *Doxology: The Praise of God in Worship, Doctrine, and Life.* New York: Oxford University Press, 1980 [especially the Introduction, chapters 7 and 8].

Weakland, Archbishop Rembert. "Active Participation: How Our Culture Affects Our Liturgy," *Church Magazine* (Spring 2001). New York: National Pastoral Life Center.

Zimmerman, Joyce Ann, et al. *Living Liturgy: Spirituality, Celebration, and Catechesis for Sundays and Solemnities (Year A, B, or C).* Collegeville: The Liturgical Press, 2001.

Chapter II

The Roman Missal
and Related Collections

⌘

THE ROMAN MISSAL
and Related Collections

Sacramentary

Lectionary for Mass
Volumes I, II, III, IV

Book of the Gospels

Lectionary for Masses with Children
Volume A, B, C: Readings for Sundays and Solemnities
Volume W: Weekday Readings

Collection of Masses for the Blessed Virgin Mary
Volume I: Sacramentary
Volume II: Lectionary

⌘

THE CHURCH'S RESOURCES: THE LITURGICAL BOOKS

In chapters II and III, the reader will be introduced to a "basic book-shelf"—the official liturgical books of the Church. Anyone who prepares liturgies must be familiar with their contents, their generous options, and their sensitivity to pastoral realities.

A brief introduction to each of these books is provided. An outline of each book is included so that you might understand the breadth of its contents and so that you may readily view the section that pertains to your particular parish celebration.

THE ROMAN MISSAL

In the early Church, those who presided over the eucharistic meal gave thanks "to the best of their ability," and read the "memoirs of the apostles" as time allowed (*First Apology of Justin Martyr*, ca. 150). Eventually, prayers were composed, written down, and shared. Ancient church orders reveal standardized prayers, laws, and rubrics for ritual. Later, prayers were gathered in "little books" called *libelli*. Ordos, usually composed for papal or episcopal liturgies, began to be circulated and adapted by local communities or entire countries.

The Missal of Pius V was developed soon after the Council of Trent and used for nearly four hundred years. Printed in Latin, it contained all the presidential prayers, the antiphons and psalms, as well as the readings. In 1963, the fathers of Vatican II called for the revision of all the Church's liturgical books. A commission called the Consilium carried out that mandate and a new Roman Missal was promulgated by Pope Paul VI in 1969. An English translation of that was approved for the USA in 1970. In this period, the Roman Missal was divided into two books—the *Sacramentary*, which contains the propers and ordinary of the Mass, and the *Lectionary*, which contains the readings assigned to the Mass of a particular day, occasion, or rite.

Pope John Paul II revised the Roman Missal yet again—the third edition since Vatican II. It is not unusual to release the *praenotanda*, or "introductory notes," before the release of a liturgical book itself. Thus, the new *General Instruction of the Roman Missal* (GIRM) was issued in the summer of 2000. Further refinements to the GIRM came in 2002. The United States bishops made adaptations to the GIRM in November 2001 and those were confirmed by CDWDS on April 17, 2002. They became particular law in the USA on April 25, 2002.

Usually, a new liturgical book is first promulgated in Latin; this is called an *editio typica* or a "typical edition." Then the conference of bishops translates the book into the language(s) of their territory. Often this may take several years from the time the *editio typica* is first released. The English translation of the *General Instruction* was confirmed by Rome on March 17, 2003, and became effective in the dioceses of the USA on March 19, 2003. At this writing, commissions are laboring on an English translation of the entire Sacramentary or Missal.

Selected Dates in the Revision of the Roman Missal

1548–1563	Council of Trent calls for the reform of the liturgical books
1570	Missal of Pius V ("Tridentine Mass")
11-20-1947	*Mediator Dei* by Pope Pius XII
1948–1960	Commission for Liturgical Reform—scholars report to Pope Pius XII
1951	Easter Vigil restored to Saturday evening
1955	Holy Week reforms
12-4-63	*Sacrosanctum Concilium,* Constitution on the Sacred Liturgy
9-26-64	*Inter Oecumenici,* guide for the implementation of the reform, calls for gradual introduction of the vernacular beginning March 7, 1965
4-3-69	*editio typica* of Roman Missal published, effective 11-30-69
3-26-70	CDW authorizes English translation of the Order of Mass for USA

The Roman Missal: The Lectionary for Mass

4-3-69	Paul VI approves the Lectionary prepared by the Consilium for the Implementation of the Constitution on the Sacred Liturgy
5-25-69	(Pentecost) *editio typica* released in one volume; conferences were to translate pericopes; could use vernacular texts from Bible translations already approved; confirmation required by Apostolic See
11-30-69	(First Sunday of Advent) Lectionary may be used; begin with Cycle B, Cycle II [Series B, II]
1-21-81	*editio typica altera* released by CDWDS
6-20-92	English translation of Volume I approved by US bishops
November 1992	remainder of Lectionary translation approved
June 1994	US bishops revoke confirmation of NAB and new Psalter
June 1997	US bishops approve a revised text of Volume I, with a proviso that it be reviewed in five years; must be used by 11-29-98
June 9, 2001	US bishops approve Volumes II, III, IV
5-19-2002	Use of revised, four volume text becomes mandatory in USA
January 2003	US bishops begin consultation for review of the Lectionary for Mass

The Roman Missal: The Sacramentary and the GIRM

4-3-69	*editio typica* of Roman Missal promulgated by Pope Paul VI
1970	revised *Ordo Missae* issued; includes the first edition of *Institutio Generalis Missalis Romani;* IGMR later revised in 1972
3-26-70	CDW authorizes English translation of Order of Mass for USA
11-13-73	NCCB approves English translation of the Sacramentary for USA

2-4-74	CDW confirms this English translation
1974	CDWDS approves English translation of Sacramentary
3-27-75	*editio typica altera* (second typical edition) of Roman Missal and the General Instruction of the Roman Missal (GIRM) promulgated
3-1-85	revisions to the RM and GIRM to reflect revised Code of Canon Law
10-6-98	US bishops submit proposed changes to US edition of Sacramentary
4-20-2000	Pope John Paul II approves revised *Institutio Generalis Missalis Romani*; published Pentecost 2000, becomes effective when published within the *editio typica* of *Missale Romanum*
July 2000	BCL (USA) releases English study edition of GIRM; ICEL edition followed but remanded for new translation after *Liturgiam Authenticam* released
3-28-01	CDWDS publishes *"Liturgiam Authenticam:* On the Use of Vernacular Languages in the Publication of the Books of the Roman Liturgy"
11-14-01	Latin Rite members of the USCCB approve adaptations to the GIRM for the dioceses of the United States
3-18-02	*Missale Romanum, editio typica tertia* published in Rome; contains slightly revised GIRM
4-17-02	CDWDS confirms US adaptations to IGMR
11-12-02	Latin Rite members of the USCCB approve [ICEL's] English translation of GIRM
3-17-03	English [ICEL] translation of IGMR, *editio typica tertia,* confirmed by CDWDS
3-19-03	USCCB publishes this version as sole translation for use in dioceses of the USA

The Roman Missal: Book of the Gospels

8-6-84	Book of the Gospels published by the authority of the BCL; arrangement of pericopes in accord with the *Ordo Lectionum Missae, editio typica altera*, 1-21-81. It uses the New American version of the Bible (approved for use in the liturgy by the NCCB in November 1968 and confirmed by the Sacred Congregation for the Rites on December 9, 1968)
November 1999	US Bishops approve vernacular edition of the Book of the Gospels
5-23-2000	CDWDS approves translation and Introduction
9-30-2000	(Feast of St. Jerome) Book of the Gospels may be used in liturgy; its use is mandatory on the First Sunday of Advent 2000

Sacramentary

The Sacramentary contains the presidential prayers and the assembly's responses. In this book you will find two types of prayers that are used in the celebration of Mass. The ordinary of the Mass are those prayers that are used at every Mass (and options for alternative texts). Here, too, you will find the complete texts for our ten eucharistic prayers and a variety of prefaces. Solemn Blessings suited to specific seasons or occasions, Prayers over the People, Latin texts, and prayers for Masses at which only one minister participates are provided.

The bulk of the Sacramentary is a collection of proper prayers for Mass, i.e., prayers that change for each celebration—antiphons, the Opening Prayer, the Prayer over the Gifts, and the Prayer after Communion. Go to the "Proper of Seasons" to find prayers for Sunday and weekday celebrations during Advent, Christmas, Lent, Holy Week, Triduum, the Easter season, Ordinary Time, and solemnities of the Lord.

The Church is always aware that every assembly prays in communion with those who have gone before us. It sets aside special days (often the anniversary of their death) to honor the saints with specific Mass texts. When celebrating the solemnity, feast, or memorial of a saint, the Church prays those orations listed in the "Proper of Saints." These are conveniently arranged from January to December.

One can also turn to less specific prayers called "Commons" which can be used in Masses for the dedication of a church or its anniversary, Masses in honor of the Blessed Virgin Mary, and Masses in honor of Martyrs, Pastors, Doctors of the Church, Virgins, and Holy Men and Women.

Ritual Masses (those in which we celebrate a rite, e.g., Baptism, Confirmation, Marriage) have their own set of proper prayers. These can be found in the section appropriately titled "Ritual Masses."

When the Church gathers to celebrate the Eucharist in other circumstances, one may turn to the section captioned "Masses for Various Needs and Occasions" to find prayers that enlist God's help "for the holy Church," "for public needs," "for various public circumstances," and "for various needs."

In addition, the Sacramentary provides prayers for votive Masses that concentrate on one saint, one title for Jesus, or one aspect of our faith. Here, you may read such titles as "The Holy Spirit" or "Jesus Christ, the Eternal High Priest."

Finally, the Church has a long tradition of praying for its deceased members. The section entitled "Masses for the Dead" contains prayers suited to various pastoral circumstances.

The appendices provide a wealth of information and additional prayers garnered from other ritual books.

The best way to appreciate the breadth of this collection is to peruse the outline that follows. Then open your copy of the Sacramentary and carefully study its contents.

Introductions/Instructions
    Decree of the Congregation for Divine Worship
    Decree of the CDW for second typical edition
    General Instruction of the Roman Missal
    Directory for Masses with Children (USA)
    Apostolic Letter of Paul VI [regarding the liturgical calendar]
    General Norms for the Liturgical Year and the Calendar
    General Roman Calendar
    Proper Calendar for the Dioceses of USA
    Table of Movable Feasts

Proper of the Seasons
    Advent Season
    Christmas Season
    Lenten Season
    Holy Week
    Easter Triduum
    Easter Season
    Ordinary Time
    Solemnities of the Lord during Ordinary Time

Order of the Mass
    Order of Mass with a Congregation
    Prefaces
    Eucharistic Prayers I, II, III, IV
    Solemn Blessings
    Prayers over the People
    Order of Mass without a Congregation

Proper of Saints
    January to December

Commons
    Dedication of a Church
    Common of the Blessed Virgin Mary
    Common of Martyrs
    Common of Pastors
    Common of Doctors of the Church

Common of Virgins
Common of Holy Men and Women
Optional Antiphons for Seasons and Feasts

Ritual Masses
Christian Initiation
Election or Enrollment of Names
The Scrutinies
Baptism
Confirmation
Holy Orders
Viaticum
Wedding Mass
Consecration to a Life of Virginity
Religious Profession

Masses and Prayers for Various Needs and Occasions
For the Church
For the Universal Church
For the Pope
For the Bishop
For the Election of a Pope or Bishop
For a Council or Synod
For Priests
For the Priest Himself
For the Ministers of the Church
For Priestly Vocations
For Religious
For Religious Vocations
For the Laity
For Unity of Christians
For the Spread of the Gospel
For Persecuted Christians
For Pastoral or Spiritual Meetings

For Civil Needs
For the Nation (State) or City
For Those Who Serve in Public Office
For the Congress
For the President
For the Progress of Peoples

        For Peace and Justice
        In Time of War or Civil Disturbance

For Various Public Needs
        Beginning of the Civil Year [Not in USA; Mary, Mother of God]
        For the Blessings of Human labor
        For Productive Land
        After the Harvest
        In Time of Famine or for Those Who Suffer from Famine
        For Refugees and Exiles
        For Those Unjustly Deprived of Liberty
        For Prisoners
        For the Sick
        For the Dying
        In Time of Earthquake
        For Rain
        For Fine Weather
        To Avert Storms
        For Any Need
        In Thanksgiving

For Particular Needs
        For Forgiveness of Sins
        For Charity
        For Promoting Harmony
        For the Family
        For Family and Friends
        For Our Oppressors
        For Happy Death

Votive Masses
        Holy Trinity
        Holy Cross
        Holy Eucharist
        Holy Name
        Precious Blood
        Sacred Heart
        Holy Spirit
        Blessed Virgin Mary
        Angels
        Joseph
        Apostles

Appendix III
>   Music for the Order of Mass

Appendix IV
>   *Ordo Missae Cum Populo*
>   *Ordo Missae Sine Populo*

Appendix V
>   Rite of Commissioning a Special Minister to Distribute Holy
>   Communion on a Single Occasion

Appendix VI
>   Eucharistic Prayers for Masses with Children (C1, C2, C3)
>   Eucharistic Prayers for Masses of Reconciliation (R1, R2)
>   Eucharistic Prayers for Masses for Various Needs and Occasions

Appendix VII
>   Anointing of the Sick during Mass

Appendix VIII
>   Dedication of a Church
>   Dedication of a Church Already in Use
>   Dedication of an Altar
>   Blessing of a Church

Appendix IX
>   Blessing of a Chalice and Paten

Appendix X
>   Additional Presidential Prayers
>   Blessing of an Abbot or Abbess
>   25th or 50th Anniversary of Religious Profession
>   For the Dying
>   Mary, Mother of the Church
>   Holy Name of Mary
>   Independence Day and Other Civic Observances

The Roman Missal of Pope John Paul II

The *Missale Romanum, editio typica tertia*, of Pope John Paul II was released in March 2002. One might expect the English translation of this liturgical book in the next few years. In it, you may find the following additions and changes to the outline found above.

For more information about the changes and additions to the *Missale Romanum*, please consult the *BCL Newsletter*, March–April 2002.

Editorial Changes

- Masses for Lent and Easter have been reordered with one setting for each day.
- Alternative formulae for various parts of the Mass have been inserted in place rather than in an appendix.
- The Eucharistic Prayers for Reconciliation and the Eucharistic Prayer for Masses for Various Needs and Occasions, though now in the center of the *editio typica,* are still in a section designated as the Appendix to the Order of Mass. The Eucharistic Prayers for Masses with Children are in Appendix VI in the back of the book, since the editors assumed that these Latin texts would not be used with children.

Changes

- Prefaces have been slightly rearranged and grouped into five categories—"Throughout the Year," "For the Feasts and Mysteries of the Lord," "For Feasts of the Saints," "For Ritual Masses," and "For Various Celebrations."
- New Prefaces—one excerpted from the Fourth Eucharistic Prayer; one from the Collection of Masses for the Blessed Virgin Mary; a second preface "For Martyrs" *(De Mirabilis Dei in Martyrium Victoria);* a preface from the revised Rite of Ordination; and a preface from the Rite of Dedication of a Church and an Altar
- A complete text of Eucharistic Prayer I (Roman Canon) with the embolisms for the Evening Mass of the Lord's Supper on Holy Thursday
- Two Solemn Blessings for the Mass of the Anointing of the Sick
- Prayers over the People for each day of the season of Lent

Additions: New Mass Sets

- For Scrutiny I, II, III
- For the Rite of Ordination
- For the Rite of Dedication of a Church and an Altar
- For the Vigil of the Ascension of the Lord
- For the Vigil of the Epiphany
- Eight new Masses from the Collection of the Masses of the BVM; these will be added into the Commons of the BVM and Votive Masses
- A second Mass set "For the Forgiveness of Sins"
- Two Mass Sets added after the "Mass for the Remission of Sins"
- Four new votive Masses—"The Mercy of God," "Our Lord Jesus Christ, Most High and Eternal Priest," "St. John the Baptist," and "Saints Peter and Paul, Apostles"

- For saints newly appointed to the Universal Calendar

St. Adalbert, bishop and martyr	April 23
St. Louis Grignon de Montfort, priest	April 28
St. Rita of Cascia	May 22
St. Peter Julian Emyard, priest	August 2
St. Maximilian Kolbe, priest and martyr	August 14
St. Peter Claver, priest	September 9
St. Andrew Kim Taegon, priest and martyr, and St. Paul Chong Hasang, catechist and martyr, and their companions, martyrs	September 20
St. Lawrence Ruiz, martyr and his companions, martyrs	September 28
St. Andrew Dung-Lac, priest and martyr, and his companions, martyrs	November 24

- Other new celebrations using current Mass sets

Most Holy Name of Jesus	January 3
St. Josephine Bakhita, virgin	February 8
Our Lady of Fatima	May 13
St. Christopher Magallenes, priest and his companions, martyrs	May 21
St. Augustine Zhao Rong, priest and his companions, Chinese martyrs	July 9
St. Appolonarius, bishop and martyr	July 20
St. Sharbel Makhluf, priest	July 24
St. Teresa Benedicta of the Cross (Edith Stein), virgin and martyr	August 9
The Most Holy Name of Mary	September 12
Martyrs of Vietnam	November 24
St. Catherine of Alexandria, virgin and martyr	November 25
St. Juan Diego	December 9

Emendations

- Rubrics of Holy Week revised in light of the 1988 *Circular Letter*

- Corrections in some prayers, e.g., Opening Prayer of 18th Sunday in Ordinary Time

- Intercessions for the bishop in the eucharistic prayers

- Antiphons brought into conformity with the texts used in the same celebrations in the *Graduale Romanum*, e.g., Common of BVM and Common of Saints

- Masses for Various Needs and Occasions now divided into three sections (instead of four)—"For the Holy Church," "For Public Circumstances," "For Various Needs"

- Masses for the Dead now divided into four sections (instead of six) "Funeral Masses," "Anniversary Mass," "Various Commemorations," and "Various Prayers for the Dead"

Lectionary for Mass

Recognizing that the word of God is central to the Church's life and liturgy, the Second Vatican Council urged that the "treasures of the Bible be opened up more lavishly so that a richer share in God's word may be provided for the faithful" (SC 51).

> [T]he liturgical celebration, based primarily on the word of God and sustained by it, becomes a new event and enriches the word itself with new meaning and power. Thus in the liturgy, the Church faithfully adheres to the way Christ himself read and explained the Scripture, beginning with the today of his coming forward in the synagogue and urging all to search the Scriptures (LMI 3).

The *Lectionary for Mass* is the liturgical book which contains the readings. Taking its title from the word *lectio* (Latin, "an act of reading"), it is a collection of readings which reflects the "heart" of the Bible, but does not contain every word of it. It contains brief pericopes (Greek, "section" or "selection") that have been carefully chosen to illuminate various facets of the paschal mystery.

Each Sunday and solemnity is assigned three readings—one from the Old Testament (except during the Easter season), the second from an apostle, and a third from one of the four gospels. The readings for Sunday are arranged in three yearly cycles. In Cycle A, we primarily (though not exclusively) read from the Gospel according to Matthew; in Cycle B, Mark; and in Cycle C, Luke. The Gospel of John is used in all three years, especially in the Easter season and to supplement the brief gospel of Mark in Year B.

The Old Testament reading nearly always "matches" the message of the gospel. In the Easter season, the Church does not read from the Old Testament, but chooses pericopes from the Acts of the Apostles. The second reading is taken from the New Testament letters or the book of Revelation. These selections are read in course during Ordinary Time, i.e., we draw from the same letter for several weeks running.

The weekday readings are divided into two annual cycles. We read Cycle I in the odd-numbered years and Cycle II in the even-numbered years. Weekday celebrations utilize one reading besides the gospel reading. For more information on the Order of Readings for Mass, see Part II of the *Introduction to the Lectionary for Mass.*

The cursus of readings is organized around the liturgical year as well as various pastoral circumstances. Each day's readings or collection of readings is assigned a "Lectionary number." You will want to use this number (and not a page number) when you and your team are preparing liturgies.

The Lectionary used in the United States has recently been revised and new translations were released 1998–2001. At this writing, a task group is consulting a broad population of bishops, liturgical scholars, and diocesan commissions to review the effectiveness of the translation and other editorial changes. In the 1994–2000 revision process, the Lectionary underwent a variety of improvements, e.g., consistent *incipits* (first lines), a more generous offering of optional readings, improved capitalization, and the use of sense lines.

Sense lines allow the priest, deacon, or lector to understand the reading more clearly and to proclaim it more effectively. The readings are no longer printed in block or paragraph form. Thus, the size of the Lectionary was impacted; it is now published in four volumes. These were gradually translated, approved, and published for use in the USA. Their use became mandatory on May 19, 2002. An outline of these four volumes may be found on the following pages.

Introduction to the Lectionary for Mass

Preamble
Part I: The Word of God in the Celebration of the Mass
Part II: The Structure of the Order of Readings for Mass
Table I: Principle Celebrations of the Liturgical Year
Table II: Order for the First Reading for Weekdays in Ordinary Time

Volume I: Sundays and Solemnities	*Lectionary #*
Sunday Readings (A, B, C)	
Advent Season	1–12
Christmas Season	13–21
Lenten Season	22–38
Chrism Mass	260
Easter Triduum	39–42
Easter Season	43–63
Octave of Easter	261–266
Season of the Year (Ordinary Time)	64–162
Alleluia Verses for Sundays in Ordinary Time	163

Volume II: Cycle I of the Seasons for Weekdays and the Complete Propers and Commons of Saints

Volume IV: Ritual Masses, Masses for Various Needs and Occasions, and Masses for the Dead

Ritual Masses

Book of the Gospels

Since the time of Gregory the Great, formal books containing readings from Sacred Scripture have been in use at Mass. Traditionally, special books containing just the gospel pericopes have been beautifully bound and ornately decorated, so that the words and deeds of Jesus Christ, as recorded by the evangelists, might be suitably adorned.

"So clearly is the Book of the Gospels a sign of Christ present in the Liturgy, that it is revered with the same holy kiss given to the altar" (BG Intro 6). It (and never the Lectionary) is borne in by the deacon or reader in procession. It is used in the ordination rites for a deacon and a bishop and enshrined at councils or synods—a sign of Christ himself as teacher and guide (ibid. 7).

It contains all the Sunday gospels for cycles A, B, and C; for the solemnities of the Lord; and for ritual Masses. The latest English edition of the *Book of the Gospels* was approved for use in the United States by the USCCB on November 16, 1999, and subsequently confirmed by the CDWDS on May 23, 2000. The sole use of this edition became mandatory in the dioceses of the USA on the First Sunday of Advent, December 3, 2000.

Decree of the Congregation for Divine Worship and Discipline of the Sacraments

Decree of the National Conference of Catholic Bishops

Introduction

Sunday Gospels

    Season of Advent

    Season of Christmas

    Season of Lent

    Easter Triduum and Season of Easter

    Ordinary Time

Solemnities and Feasts of the Lord and of the Saints

    Solemnities of the Lord During Ordinary Time
        The Most Holy Trinity
        The Most Holy Body and Blood of Christ
        The Most Sacred Heart of Jesus

    Chrism Mass

    Octave of Easter

February 2	Presentation of the Lord
March 19	St. Joseph, Husband of the BVM
March 25	Annunciation of the Lord
June 24	Nativity of St. John the Baptist
June 29	Saints Peter and Paul, Apostles
August 6	Transfiguration of the Lord
August 15	Assumption of the BVM
September 14	Exaltation of the Holy Cross
November 1	All Saints
November 2	Commemoration of All the Faithful Departed
November 9	Dedication of the Lateran Basilica
December 8	Immaculate Conception of the BVM
December 12	Our Lady of Guadalupe

Ritual Masses

Admittance into the Catechumenate

The Presentation of the Creed

The Presentation of the Lord's Prayer

Christian Initiation apart from Easter Vigil

Conferral of Infant Baptism

Confirmation

Holy Orders

Admission to Candidacy for the Diaconate and the Priesthood

Institution of Readers

Institution of Acolytes

Anointing of the Sick

Marriage

Blessing of an Abbott and an Abbess

Consecration to a Life of Virginity and Religious Profession

Dedication of a Church

Dedication of an Altar

The Blessing of a Chalice and a Paten

Lectionary for Masses with Children

From the time of their baptism, the Church must exercise a special care for children. This is especially true as we welcome these children into our liturgical assemblies. The *Directory for Masses with Children* (CDWDS, 1973), a supplement to the *General Instruction of the Roman Missal*, reveals this special care and offers practical ways to adapt liturgies to the needs of children.

As a direct result of a formal position statement passed by the Federation of Diocesan Liturgical Commissions, the United States Conference of Bishops commissioned a translation of the *Lectionary for Mass* suitable for children. The vocabulary was to be geared toward a preadolescent's reading level and comprehension.

The *Lectionary for Masses with Children* was prepared by a task group of the Bishops' Committee on the Liturgy. Made up of experts in liturgy, Scripture, and catechetics, the task group examined lectionaries for children in other languages, composed a new Introduction, and compiled a simplified cursus of readings. Their work was approved by the NCCB on November 13, 1991. In a decree dated December 28, 1992 (appropriately, the feast of the Holy Innocents), the NCCB ruled that the effective date for the LMC's use in the dioceses of the US would be the First Sunday of Advent 1993.

Earlier, on May 27, 1992, the Congregation for Divine Worship and Discipline of the Sacraments had granted "permission for experimental use of the cursus of the *Lectionary for Masses with Children*." After a three-year period a full report was to be given and a renewal or definite confirmation was to be sought. The Congregation laid down several terms for this permission. First, the LMC was not to be used at Sunday Masses even when large numbers of children were present. Second, "no approved version of scripture is *a priori* excluded from use." Third, on Christmas, Epiphany, the Sundays of Lent, Easter Sunday, Ascension, and Pentecost, the NCCB was to add a rubric announcing preference for the readings in the *Lectionary for Mass.* Finally, "on the basis of the assurance given that the CEV [Contemporary English Version] of the Bible does not present any doctrinal problems in the sphere of issue of inclusive language at present under study we grant permission for its experimental use but without granting a formal confirmation."

The task force had chosen the American Bible Society's Contemporary English Version of the Bible for the readings from the Old Testament, New Testament, the book of Psalms, and a number of refrains for the responsorial psalms. English translations of the titles of the readings, psalm responses, Alleluia verses, Lenten acclamations, and verses before the gospel were taken from ICEL's translation of the *Lectionary for Mass.*

The LMC was released in four volumes—A, B, C, and Weekdays. It does not contain readings for the days of the Triduum. On Christmas, Epiphany, the Sundays of Lent, Easter, Ascension, and Pentecost preference is given to the *Lectionary for Mass.*

The Introduction is important reading for anyone who prepares Masses with children. Several points should be noted. First (as the CDWDS had cautioned), the LMC is not to be used at Sunday Mass even when large numbers of children are present (13). Second, while a separate Liturgy of the Word for children, apart from the Sunday assembly, is permitted, it should be occasional "to protect the domestic church" (14). Third, when preparing liturgies with children, it is permissible to use two readings or only one reading, but the reading of the gospel is never omitted (16). When a reading from the *Lectionary for Mass* was deemed inappropriate for children, it was omitted and not replaced by another (19).

Perhaps the most memorable advice to presiders, catechists, and others who work with our youngest parishioners can be found in paragraph twenty-one of the Introduction: "The liturgy has the power to form children and all believers in the paschal mystery. The worthy celebration of the liturgy itself is the best introduction to liturgy."

Toward that end, the Bishops' Committee on the Liturgy offered this *Lectionary for Masses with Children* to "enable children to hear the word of God in a manner more suited to their age and ability to understand. In providing this lectionary it is our sincere desire to enable young children to come to Christ, from whom they have received new life in baptism and who gives them the joy of salvation" (Bishop Wilton Gregory, chairman of the BCL, Foreword).

As noted above, in 1992 the LMC was approved only for experimental use. A task force of the BCL has been reviewing the LMC since 2002.

At the June 2003 meeting of the USCCB, the bishops made significant changes to the Introduction. The resultant text is more in harmony with the *Directory for Masses with Children.*

The task group has decided not to use the Contemporary English Version of the Bible, but to make adaptations to the New American Bible translation.

Volumes A, B, and C: Readings for Sundays and Solemnities

Decree of the NCCB

Decree of the CDWDS

Foreword

Introduction
The Liturgical Celebration of the Word (1–5)
The Celebration of the Word of God with Children (6–10)
The Lectionary for Masses with Children
a. One Lectionary (11–14)
b. Adapted for Particular Hearers of the Word (15–20)
c. That the Word of God Might Be Proclaimed in the
Liturgical Celebration (21–24)
d. Throughout the Liturgical Year (25–48)
Particular Issues
Conclusion

Sunday Readings
Season of Advent
Season of Christmas
Season of Lent
Season of Easter
Ordinary Time

Solemnities of the Lord During Ordinary Time

Common Texts for Responsorial Psalms

Calendar

Index of Readings

Volume W: Weekday Readings

Decree of the NCCB

Decree of the CDWDS

Foreword

Introduction

Weekday Readings
Season of Advent
Season of Lent
Season of Easter
Ordinary Time
Gospel Acclamations for Weekdays in Ordinary Time

Proper of Saints (January to December)

Commons
> Common of the Dedication of a Church
> Common of the BVM
> Common of the Apostles
> Common of Martyrs
> Common of Pastors
> Common of the Doctors of the Church
> Common of Saints

Sacraments
> Baptism
> Confirmation (Holy Spirit)
> Holy Eucharist
> Reconciliation

Masses for Various Needs and Occasions
> Beginning of the School Year
> End of the School Year
> In Thanksgiving
> For Vocations
> For the Unity of Christians
> For Peace and Justice
> For Productive Land and After the Harvest
> For Refugees and Exiles
> For the Sick
> For the Dead

Calendar

Index of Readings

Collectio Missarum de Beata Maria Virgine

Collection of Masses for the Blessed Virgin Mary

Volume I: Sacramentary

Volume II: Lectionary

In response to requests from pastors, the faithful, and rectors of Marian shrines, the Congregation for Divine Worship published a collection of Masses that honored the Blessed Virgin Mary and fostered devotion to her. They selected orations from existing Mass formularies. In addition, they chose new texts that had been composed by particular Churches and religious institutes (Decree of the CDW, August 15, 1986). "These Masses were created on the basis of the study of ancient liturgical sources and of the writings of the Fathers of the Church of both the East and the West, on an examination of the Church's magisterium, and on a judicious balancing of the old and the new" (ibid.).

The *editio typica* was promulgated on the Solemnity of the Assumption in 1986. A translation was prepared by ICEL and was approved for use in the United States of America by the NCCB on September 27, 1989. Confirmation came from the CDW on March 20, 1990, and the effective date for its use in the USA was December 8, 1992.

The collection is published in two volumes. Volume I is a Sacramentary that contains euchological texts, entrance and Communion antiphons, and an appendix with formularies for solemn blessings. Volume II is a Lectionary that includes readings assigned to each Mass, the responsorial psalms, and the alleluia verse or verse before the gospel.

The collection is arranged according to the liturgical year, beginning with the seasons of Advent, Christmas, Lent, and Easter. The formularies for Ordinary Time are divided into three sections. First, there are eleven formularies that focus on titles of Mary found in Sacred Scripture or that express Mary's role in the life of the Church. Second, there are nine formularies based upon Mary's titles as one who fosters the spiritual life of the faithful. Third, there are eight formularies that suggest her compassionate intercession on behalf of the faithful.

These Masses may be used at Marian shrines where Masses for the BVM are celebrated frequently, at Masses celebrated on a pilgrimage, or at Masses for the benefit of people on a pilgrimage. They may be used anywhere on any Saturday in Ordinary Time when not impeded by an obligatory memorial. As long as the liturgical year is respected, this collection may be used on any day except nos. 1–6 of the Table of Liturgical Days. During the seasons of Advent, Christmas, Lent, and Easter, and the feasts therein, the biblical readings are those assigned in the *Lectionary for Mass* (cf. General Introduction, nos. 27–37).

In his foreword to the US edition, Bishop Wilton Gregory noted that "this collection of Masses in honor of the BVM is a witness to the many ways and reasons Christians have honored Mary. These Masses are a meditation on the history of our salvation in Christ and the very nature of the Christian life. Through the use of this resource of Scripture, prayer, and praise may we join Mary in proclaiming the greatness of the Lord and ever rejoicing in God our Savior."

Volume I: Sacramentary

Decree of the National Conference of Catholic Bishops
Decree of the Congregation for Divine Worship and Discipline
   of the Sacraments
Foreword

General Introduction

Advent Season

1. The Blessed Virgin Mary, Chosen Daughter of Israel
2. The Blessed Virgin Mary and the Annunciation of the Lord
3. The Visitation of the Blessed Virgin Mary

Christmas Season

4. Holy Mary, Mother of God
5. The Blessed Virgin Mary, Mother of the Savior
6. The Blessed Virgin Mary and the Epiphany of the Lord
7. The Blessed Virgin Mary and the Presentation of the Lord
8. Our Lady of Nazareth
9. Our Lady of Cana

Lenten Season

10. Holy Mary, Disciple of the Lord
11. The Blessed Virgin Mary at the Foot of the Cross, I
12. The Blessed Virgin Mary at the Foot of the Cross, II
13. The Commending of the Blessed Virgin Mary
14. The Blessed Virgin Mary, Mother of Reconciliation

Easter Season

15. The Blessed Virgin Mary and the Resurrection of the Lord
16. Holy Mary, Fountain of Light and Life

17. Our Lady of the Cenacle
18. The Blessed Virgin Mary, Queen of Apostles

Order of the Mass

Prefaces (#1–50)
Eucharistic Prayer I or Roman Canon
Eucharistic Prayer II
Eucharistic Prayer III
Eucharistic Prayer IV
Appendix: Solemn Blessings
 Advent, Christmas, Lent, Easter, Ordinary Time (3)

Ordinary Time

Section 1

19. Holy Mary, Mother of the Lord
20. Holy Mary, the New Eve
21. The Holy Name of the Blessed Virgin Mary
22. Holy Mary, Handmaid of the Lord
23. The Blessed Virgin Mary, Temple of the Lord
24. The Blessed Virgin Mary, Seat of Wisdom
25. The Blessed Virgin Mary, Image and Mother of the Church, I
26. The Blessed Virgin Mary, Image and Mother of the Church, II
27. The Blessed Virgin Mary, Image and Mother of the Church, III
28. The Immaculate Heart of the Blessed Virgin Mary
29. The Blessed Virgin Mary, Queen of All Creation

Section 2

30. The Blessed Virgin Mary, Mother and Mediatrix of Grace
31. The Blessed Virgin Mary, Fountain of Salvation
32. The Blessed Virgin Mary, Mother and Teacher in the Spirit
33. The Blessed Virgin Mary, Mother of Good Counsel
34. The Blessed Virgin Mary, Cause of Our Joy
35. The Blessed Virgin Mary, Pillar of Faith
36. The Blessed Virgin Mary, Mother of Fairest Love
37. The Blessed Virgin Mary, Mother of Divine Hope
38. Holy Mary, Mother of Unity

Section 3

39. Holy Mary, Queen and Mother of Mercy
40. The Blessed Virgin Mary, Mother of Divine Providence
41. The Blessed Virgin Mary, Mother of Consolation
42. The Blessed Virgin Mary, Help of Christians

FOR FURTHER READING

The Sacramentary and the Lectionary for Mass

Cabié, Robert. *The Eucharist*. Trans. Matthew J. O'Connell. The Church at Prayer: An Introduction to the Liturgy, Volume II. Collegeville: The Liturgical Press, 1986.

Connell, Martin. *Guide to the Revised Lectionary*. Archdiocese of Chicago: Liturgy Training Publications, 1998.

Mazza, Enrico. *The Eucharistic Prayers of the Roman Rite*. Trans. Matthew J. O'Connell. New York: Pueblo Publishing Company, 1986.

McCarron, Richard. *The Eucharistic Prayer at Sunday Mass*. Archdiocese of Chicago: Liturgy Training Publications, 1997.

Palazzo, Eric. *A History of Liturgical Books from the Beginning to the Thirteenth Century*. Trans. Madeleine Beaumont. Collegeville: The Liturgical Press, 1998.

Seasoltz, Kevin. *New Liturgy, New Laws*. Collegeville: The Liturgical Press, 1980.

Secretariat for the Liturgy, USCCB. "Presentation of Oils to the Parish," *BCL Newsletter*, Volume XXVI (March 1990) 10–11.

———. *Pastoral Introduction for the Order of Mass*. Washington, D.C.: USCCB, 2003.

White, James. *Documents of Christian Worship: Descriptive and Interpretive Sources*. Louisville, Ky.: Westminster/John Knox Press, 1992.

Lectionary for Masses with Children

Bernstein, Eleanor and John Brooks-Leonard, eds. *Children in the Assembly of the Church*. Archdiocese of Chicago: Liturgy Training Publications, 1992.

Congregation for Divine Worship and Discipline of the Sacraments. *Directory for Masses with Children*, 1973.

Mazar, Peter, and Robert Piercy. *A Guide to the Lectionary for Masses with Children*. Chicago: Archdiocese of Chicago: Liturgy Training Publications, 1993.

"The New LMC: What It Is and How It Affects Your Ministry," a 1993 supplement to *Liturgy 90*. Archdiocese of Chicago: Liturgy Training Publications, 1993.

Publishers

The *Lectionary for Mass* is published by the following companies with the permission of the USCCB:

Chicago: Archdiocese of Chicago, Liturgy Training Publications (Volume I in separate ritual books for Cycles A, B, and C; Volume II; Volume III, Volume IV; also available in a paperback study edition in Volume I and Volume II–IV). 1-800-933-1800. www.ltp.org.

Collegeville, Minnesota: Liturgical Press (Volumes I–IV, ceremonial edition, classic edition, chapel edition, study edition, and loose-leaf study edition) 1-800-858-5450. www.litpress.org.

Totowa, N.J.: Catholic Book Publishing.

The *Book of the Gospels* is available from the following publishers:

Archdiocese of Chicago: Liturgy Training Publications.

Collegeville: Liturgical Press (0-8146-2572-X). 1-800-858-5450. www.litpress.org.

Totowa, N.J.: Catholic Book Publishing.

The *Lectionary for Masses with Children* is available from the following publishers:

Archdiocese of Chicago: Liturgy Training Publications (study and ritual editions available in four volumes). 1-800-933-1800. www.ltp.org.

Liturgical Press (Pueblo Books Edition) 0-1-8146-6139-6 (ritual edition). 1-800-858-5450. www.litpress.org.

Chapter III

Other Liturgical Books

⌘

THE ROMAN RITUAL

Rites of Initiation
>   Rite of Christian Initiation of Adults (1974, 1988)
>   Rite of Reception of Baptized Christians into the Full
>   Communion of the Catholic Church (1988)
>   Rite of Baptism for Children (1969, 1973)
>   Rite of Confirmation (1973)
Rite of Penance (1973)
Rite of Marriage (1969, 1990)
Book of Blessings (1989)
Pastoral Care of the Sick (1974, 1983 USA)
>   Rite of Anointing and Viaticum
Order of Christian Funerals (1989)
Holy Communion and Worship of the Eucharist outside Mass (1973)
Order for the Solemn Exposition of the Holy Eucharist (USA 1992)
Rite of Blessing of Oils, Consecration of Chrism (1970)

ROMAN PONTIFICAL

Rite of Dedication of a Church and an Altar (1989)
Rite of Confirmation (1973)
Rite of Ordination (2003)
>   Of a Bishop
>   Of Priests
>   Of Deacons
>   Of Deacons and Priests in the Same Celebration
>   Rite of Admission to Candidacy for Ordination as Deacons
>   and Priests
Other Rites in the Pontifical
>   Institution of Ministers and the Blessing of Persons
>   Blessing of Persons (incorporated into the *Book of
>   Blessings*, 1989)
>   Consecration to a Life of Virginity
>   Rite of Religious Profession
>   For Men
>   For Women
>   Blessing of Abbots and Abbesses
>   Blessing of Objects and Places
>   Blessing of Papal Insignia

Order of Crowning an Image of the Blessed Virgin Mary
(March 25, 1985)

LITURGY OF THE HOURS

SUNDAY CELEBRATIONS IN THE ABSENCE OF A PRIEST (USA)

⌘

THE ROMAN RITUAL

In addition to the books used at Mass, the Second Vatican Council mandated that each ritual book would be restored "to impart an ever-increasing vigor to the Christian life of the faithful, to adapt more suitably to the needs of our own times, . . . to foster whatever can promote union among all who believe in Christ, and . . . to call the whole of humanity into the household of the Church" (SC 1). In short, the goal of the reform of the liturgy was to reform the Church.

Not since 1614 had the *Roman Ritual* undergone such a thorough and meaningful reform. Over the course of several years, each rite would undergo changes that would (1) express more clearly the theology inherent in each sacrament or other ritual, (2) meet pastoral realities, and (3) be in harmony with the Roman tradition of "noble simplicity." The *praenotanda* of each rite, too, would be updated to reflect more current theological, biblical, and historical research.

The *Roman Ritual* includes those books that are used for the celebration of the sacraments, funerals, Communion outside Mass, and various blessings. The following pages will give you a brief introduction to each rite and an outline of its content in order that you may more intelligently select and utilize the rite most appropriate to your celebration.

Rites of Initiation

First among the rites to be revised by the council were those pertaining to initiation.

> The Catechumenate for Adults, divided into several stages, is to be restored and put into use at the discretion of the local Ordinary. By this means, the time of the Catechumenate, which is intended as a period of well-suited instruction, may be sanctified by sacred rites to be celebrated at successive intervals of time (SC 64).

The council called for other rites of initiation to be restored or created—the Rite of Baptism for Children (SC 67–69), a rite for those already baptized in another Christian community (SC 69), and the Rite of Confirmation (SC 71).

Rite of Christian Initiation of Adults

The first edition of the RCIA was promulgated in 1974. Several editions followed, refined over the years by academic research and pastoral practice. The final edition approved for use for the diocese of the USA was promulgated in 1988.

In most parishes in the USA who have both catechumens and candidates, one will be using the combined rites, always maintaining careful distinctions between unbaptized catechumens, those baptized in other Christian communities, and baptized but uncatechized Catholics. These combined rites are found in the US Appendix to the RCIA beginning with paragraph #505. For more information on choosing the right rite, please see the chart on pages 196 and 197.

Christian Initiation: General Introduction (1–35)

Introduction (1–35)

Part I: Christian Initiation of Adults

   Period of Evangelization and Precatechumenate (36–40)

   First Step: Acceptance into the Order of Catechumens (41–74)

      Receiving the Candidates
      Liturgy of the Word
      Liturgy of the Eucharist
      Optional Rites

   Period of the Catechumenate (75–80)

   Rites Belonging to the Period of the Catechumenate

      Celebrations of the Word of God (81–89)
      Minor Exorcisms (90–94)
      Blessing of the Catechumens (95–97)
      Anointing of the Catechumens (98–103)
      Presentations (optional) (104–105)
      Sending of the Catechumens for Election (Optional) (106–117)

   Second Step: Election or Enrollment of Names (118–137)

      Liturgy of the Word
      Liturgy of the Eucharist

   Period of Purification and Enlightenment (138–140)

   Rites Belonging to the Period of Purification and Enlightenment

      The Scrutinies (141–146)

Preparation of Uncatechized Adults for Confirmation and Eucharist (400–410)

Optional Rites for Baptized but Uncatechized Adults
A. Rite of Welcoming the Candidate (411–433)
B. Rite of Sending the Candidates for Recognition by the
   Bishop and for the Call to Continuing Conversion (434–445)
C. Rite of Calling the Candidates to Continuing Conversion
   (446–458)
D. Penitential Rite (459–472)

Reception of the Baptized Christians into the Full Communion of the Catholic Church (473–504)

Reception within Mass (487–498)
Reception outside Mass (499–504)

Appendix I: Additional (Combined) Rites

Rite 1. Celebration of the Rite of Acceptance into the Order of Catechumens and of the Rite of Welcoming Baptized but Previously Uncatechized Adults Who Are Preparing for Confirmation and/or Eucharist or Reception into the Full Communion of the Catholic Church (505–529)

Rite 2. Parish Celebration for Sending Catechumens for Election and Candidates for Recognition by the Bishop (Optional) (530–546)

Rite 3. Celebration of the Rite of Election of Catechumens and of the Call to Continuing Conversion of Candidates Who Are Preparing for Confirmation and/or Eucharist or Reception into the Full Communion of the Catholic Church (547–561)

Rite 4. Celebration at the Easter Vigil of the Sacraments of Initiation and of the Rite of Reception into the Full Communion of the Catholic Church (562–594)

Appendix II: Acclamations, Hymns, and Songs

Acclamations from Sacred Scripture
Hymns in the Style of the New Testament
Songs from Ancient Liturgies

Appendix III: National Statutes for the Catechumenate

Rite of Baptism for Children

Over the centuries, especially when faced with high infant mortality rates, a children's baptismal rite developed which was brief—an adaptation of the baptism of an adult in danger of death. In 1963, the Second Vatican Council called for a fuller ritual. Further, it responded to pastoral realities by offering a rite for several children, for one child, for a great number of children, and for a rite administered by someone other than a priest or deacon (particularly useful in mission territories).

These rites may be celebrated outside Mass or within Mass. Ideally they should be celebrated at Sunday Mass in the midst of the Christian assembly. When the rite is performed within Mass, the presider may choose to use parts of the rite at appropriate times during the Mass, e.g., the "Reception of the Child" during the Introductory Rites and the "Celebration of the Sacrament" and the "Explanatory Rites" after the homily.

I. Rite of Baptism for Several Children
    Reception of the Children (32–43)
    Liturgy of the Word (44–52)
    Celebration of the Sacrament (53–61)
    Explanatory Rites (62–66)
    Conclusion of the Rite (67–71)

II. Rite of Baptism for One Child
    Reception of the Child (72–80)
    Liturgy of the Word (81–89)
    Celebration of the Sacrament (90–97)
    Explanatory Rites (98–101)
    Conclusion of the Rite (102–106)

III. Rite of Baptism for a Large Number of Children
    Reception of the Children (107–111)
    Liturgy of the Word (112–116)
    Celebration of the Sacrament (117–124)
    Explanatory Rites (125–127)
    Conclusion of the Rite (128–131)

IV. Rite of Baptism for Children Administered by a Catechist When No Deacon or Priest Is Present
    Reception of the Children (132–136)
    Liturgy of the Word (137–140)
    Celebration of the Sacrament (141–150)
    Explanatory Rites (151–153)
    Conclusion of the Rite (154–156)

Rite of Confirmation

In the early Church, the initiation rite(s) were celebrated at the same time, usually on the vigil of Easter. While space does not permit a complete historical survey, suffice it to say that the Western Church saw a dissolution of its initiation practice into three separate sacraments—baptism, confirmation, and Eucharist. The restoration of the catechumenate and the revised RCIA seek to rekindle the earlier understanding of initiation.

But pastoral reality also dictates that the Church have a distinct rite for the conferral of the sacrament of confirmation alone for those who were baptized as infants. Just as the Spirit appeared at the baptism of Jesus at the River Jordan and brought his mission to fulfillment, so too, the Church sees the sacrament of confirmation as a strengthening and completion of the sacrament of baptism.

> In the sacrament of Confirmation the apostles and the bishops, who are their successors, hand on to the baptized the special gift of the Holy Spirit, promised by Christ the Lord and poured out upon the apostles at Pentecost. Thus the initiation in the Christian life is completed so that believers are strengthened by the power from heaven, made true witnesses of Christ in word and deed, and bound more closely to the Church. To make the intimate connection of this sacrament with the whole of Christian initiation (SC 71) clearer, Vatican Council II decreed that the rite of confirmation was to be revised (Decree, CDW, 8-22-71).

This revised rite became effective on January 1, 1973, and each chapter of it responds to various pastoral circumstances—a rite within Mass and outside of it, a rite of confirmation by a minister who is not a bishop, and a rite for a person in danger of death. Finally, chapter V contains a selection of orations and readings for the celebration(s).

The renewal of baptismal promises is part of the rite (both within and outside of Mass). Then, the bishop lays hands (by extending his hands) and asks God to give the candidates the seven gifts of the Holy Spirit. Next, he continues the ancient practice of anointing with oil (chrism) and the laying on of hands. What is the actual "matter and form" of this sacrament?

> The sacrament of confirmation is conferred through the anointing with chrism on the forehead, which is done by the laying on of the hand, and through the words: Be sealed with the Gift of the Holy Spirit. But the laying of hands, carried out with the prescribed prayer before the anointing [nos. 24–25], is still to be regarded as very important, even if it is not the essence of the sacramental rite: it contributes to the complete perfection of the rite and to a more thorough understanding of the sacrament. It is evident that this prior laying on of hands differs from the later laying on of the hand in the anointing of the forehead.
> —Pope Paul VI, *Apostolic Constitution on the Sacrament of Confirmation*, 1972.

One might argue that the Rite of Confirmation is more properly placed in the Pontifical, since it is a rite at which the bishop usually presides. But a priest may also confer this sacrament and indeed ought to do so when this sacrament is conferred along with adult baptism and with the Rite of Reception into Full Communion.

I. Rite of Confirmation within Mass

>Liturgy of the Word (20)
>Sacrament of Confirmation (21–30)
>Presentation of Candidates
>>Homily
>>Renewal of Baptismal Promises
>>Laying on of Hands
>>Anointing with Chrism
>>General Intercessions
>Liturgy of the Eucharist (31–32)
>Blessing and Prayer over the People (33)

II. Rite of Confirmation outside Mass

>Entrance Rite (34–35)
>>Song
>>Opening Prayer
>Celebration of the Word of God
>Sacrament of Confirmation (38–49)
>>Presentation of Candidates
>>Homily
>>Renewal of Baptismal Promises
>>Laying on of Hands
>>Anointing with Chrism
>>General Intercessions

III. Rite of Confirmation by a Minister Who Is Not a Bishop (50–51)

IV. Confirmation of a Person in Danger of Death (52–56)

V. Texts for the Celebration of Confirmation (57–65)

Rite of Penance

> Reconciliation between God and his people was brought about by our Lord Jesus Christ in the mystery of his death and resurrection (Romans 5:10). The Lord entrusted the ministry of reconciliation to the Church in the person of the apostles (2 Cor 5:18ff.). The Church carries out this ministry . . . by baptizing . . . with water and the Holy Spirit. . . . Because of human weakness, however, Christians break off their fellowship with God by sinning. The Lord, therefore instituted a special sacrament of penance for the pardon of sins committed after baptism . . . (Decree, SCDW, 1973).

The decree that promulgated the revised *Rite of Penance* clearly expresses the nature and effect of this sacrament. Moreover, it manifests the reconciling role of the Church.

Three rites are offered in the first three chapters. First, there is a *Rite of Reconciliation of Individual Penitents*. This rite is used by a confessor and penitent in a one-on-one situation. The penitent's inner conversion and the Church's ministry of reconciliation is expressed in four basic elements—contrition, confession, an act of penance, and absolution from sin.

The second is a communal service set within a Celebration of the Word. Here, the assembled Church recognizes the impact of sin on both the individual and the community. This rite is called the *Rite of Reconciliation of Several Penitents with Individual Confession and Absolution*.

Similarly, the third rite is communal in nature, allowing for a general confession and absolution in case of grave emergency or when the number of penitents is exceedingly large. The use of this last rite has been curtailed in recent years so that penitents might make greater use of individual confession.

Chapter IV provides optional orations and readings for the above rites. Appendices offer texts for absolution from censures, sample penance services, and a form of an examination of conscience.

I. Rite of Reconciliation of Individual Penitents (41–47)

Reception of the Penitent
[Reading of the Word of God]
Confessions of Sin and Acceptance of Satisfaction
Prayer of Penitent
Absolution
Proclamation of Praise of God
Dismissal

II. Rite of Reconciliation of Several Penitents with Individual Confession and Absolution

III. Rite of Reconciliation of Several Penitents with General Confession and Absolution (60–66)

IV. Various Texts used in the Celebration of Reconciliation (67–219)

Appendix I. Absolution from Censures

Appendix II. Sample Penance Service—Lent and Advent

Appendix III. Form of Examination of Conscience

Rite of Marriage

> In virtue of the sacrament of marriage, married Christians signify and share
> in the mystery of the unity and fruitful love that exists between Christ and his
> Church; they thus help each other to attain holiness in their married life and
> in welcoming and rearing children; and they have their own special place and
> gift among the people of God. . . . To make the indissoluble marriage cove-
> nant a clearer sign of this full meaning and a surer help in its fulfillment,
> Christ raised it to the dignity of a sacrament, modeled on his own nuptial
> bond with the Church (RM 1, 2).

The revised *Rite of Marriage* (1969) actually provides three rites for the wedding liturgy of a Catholic person. First, the *Rite for Celebrating Marriage During Mass* situates the rite between the Liturgy of the Word and the Liturgy
of the Eucharist. The Lectionary and Sacramentary provide orations and
readings for this ritual Mass. They are also included in chapter IV.

The *Rite for Celebrating Marriage outside Mass* is properly used in a marriage between a Catholic and a baptized person who is not a Catholic (RM
8). If the local ordinary gives permission, the Rite of Marriage within Mass
may be used in this circumstance.

The *Rite for Celebrating Marriage between a Catholic and an Unbaptized Person* is provided in chapter III.

The choice of day and readings are detailed in no. 11 and the preparation of local customs are addressed in nos. 12–16.

A translation of the revised Rite of Marriage has been prepared for the
USA and is awaiting confirmation in Rome.

I. Rite for Celebrating Marriage within Mass (19–38)

    Entrance Rite (19–20)
    Liturgy of the Word (21–22)
    Rite of Marriage (23–29)
        Introduction
        Questions
        Consent
        Blessing of Rings
        Exchange of Rings
        General Intercessions
    Liturgy of the Eucharist (30–36)
        Nuptial Blessing (33–34)
    Concluding Rite (37–38)

II. Rite for Celebrating Marriage outside Mass (39–54)

> Entrance Rite
> Liturgy of the Word
> Rite of Marriage
>> Introduction
>> Questions
>> Consent
>> Blessing of Rings
>> Exchange of Rings
>> General Intercessions
>> Nuptial Blessing
> Conclusion of the Celebration
>> Lord's Prayer and Blessing

III. Rite for Celebrating Marriage between a Catholic and an Unbaptized Person (55–66)

> Rite of Welcome
> Liturgy of the Word
>> Readings
>> Homily
> Rite of Marriage
>> Introduction
>> Questions
>> Consent
>> Blessing of Rings
>> Exchange of Rings
>> General Intercessions
>> Nuptial Blessing
> Conclusion of the Celebration
>> Lord's Prayer and Blessing

IV. Texts for Use in the Marriage Rite and in the Wedding Mass (67–127)

Book of Blessings

The *Book of Blessings* (BB) contains the Roman volume, *De benedictionibus* (1985) and forty-two original blessings composed by the Bishops' Committee on the Liturgy and approved by the USCCB and the CDW. The blessings are divided into six major categories:

1) Blessings Pertaining to Persons
2) Blessings Related to Buildings and Human Activity
3) Blessings of Objects for Use in Churches
4) Blessings of Articles to Foster Devotion
5) Blessings Related to Feasts and Seasons
6) Blessings for Various Needs and Occasions

The USA appendices contain prayers for the Installation of a Pastor, Solemn Blessings, and Prayers over the People.

God always blesses his people "with his divine help, a proclamation of his favor, and a reassurance of his faithfulness . . . " (BBGI 6). When we invoke God's blessing, we call down God's protection; we praise and thank God for what he has already given us and ask him to continue to bless us with his bountiful goodness.

Blessings are liturgical prayers that flow from the word of God. Each blessing follows a basic form—(1) an Introductory Rite; (2) reading(s) of the Word of God and intercessory prayer(s); (3) a Prayer of Blessing; and (4) a Concluding Rite. Even shorter forms of the rite will retain nos. 2 and 4, since Scripture and the Prayer of Blessing are inherent to the rite (cf. *Book of Blessings:* General Introduction, Chapter III).

A Guide to the Chart

The chart on the following pages summarizes the content of the *Book of Blessings*. An "X" notes when the BB offers a blessing outside Mass, within Mass and/or a shorter rite. When a "W" appears in a column, it means that the BB provides a blessing within a Celebration of the Word. This is especially appropriate when you are blessing catechists, missionaries, or others who will spread the Gospel. Some blessings should never be conducted within Mass and those are so noted with the word "never."

Since a blessing, like all liturgy, is an exercise of the priestly office of Jesus Christ and all the baptized share in this priestly office, BB allows a wide variety of ministers to preside at many of the blessings. Thus the "proper minister" is noted in the last column. A bishop may be the proper minister of any of the blessings in this book. When only he can offer a blessing, a "B" appears. Other ministers include: "P" = priest; "D" = deacon; "L" = layperson; [L] = a layperson only when a bishop, priest, or deacon cannot be present;

"Parents" = the minister(s) for this blessing may be the parents of the child or the engaged couple; "C" = catechist; "Inst." = head of an institute.

BLESSINGS DIRECTLY PERTAINING TO PERSONS				
Blessing of	**Outside Mass**	**Within Mass**	**Shorter Rite**	**Proper Minister**
Family	X	X		P D L
Families in Their Homes	X			P D
Married Couple	X	X	X	P D [L]
On Anniversary		X		P
On Other Occasions		X		
Children			X	P D L
Baptized	X			
Not Yet Baptized	X			
Sons and Daughters	X			P D Parents
Engaged Couple	X			P D L Parents
Parents before Childbirth	X		X	P D L
Mother before Childbirth	X		X	P D L
Mother after Childbirth	X		X	P D L
Parents after Miscarriage	X		X	P D L
Parents and an Adopted Child	X			P D L
Occasion of a Birthday	X		X	P D L
Elderly People Confined to Homes	X	X	X	P D L
With Communion outside Mass	X			P D L
The Sick			X	P D L
Adults	X			P D L
Children	X			P D L
Persons Suffering from Addiction	X		X	P D L

continued

BLESSINGS DIRECTLY PERTAINING TO PERSONS (CONTINUED)				
Blessing of	**Outside Mass**	**Within Mass**	**Shorter Rite**	**Proper Minister**
Victim of Crime or Oppression	X		X	P D L
Missionaries Sent to Proclaim the Gospel	W	X		B P
Those Appointed as Catechists	W	X		P D
For a Catechetical or Prayer Meeting	X			P D L
Catechumens (RCIA 95–97)	X			P D C
Students and Teachers	W	X	X	P D L
Those Gathered at a Meeting				P D L
Prayers for Meetings	X			
Ecumenical Groups	X			
Interfaith Gatherings	X			
Organizations Concerned with Public Need	X			P D
Pilgrims—Departure, Return	X			P D
Travelers	X		X	P D L

BLESSINGS RELATED TO BUILDINGS AND VARIOUS FORMS OF HUMAN ACTIVITY				
Blessing of	**Outside Mass**	**Within Mass**	**Shorter Rite**	**Proper Minister**
New Building Site	X			P D
New Homes (Occupants)	X			P D L
New Seminary	X			B P
New Religious House	X			B P S
New School or University	X	X		P D
New Library	X			P D
New Parish Hall/Catechetical Ctr.	X			P D
New Hospital/ Facility for Sick	X			P D
Office, Shop, or Factory	X			P D
Centers of Social Communication	X			P D
Gymnasium or Athletic Fields	X			P D
Various Means of Transportation	X		X	P D L
Boats (Fleets) and Fishing Gear	X		X	P D L
Technical Installations/Equipment	X			P D L
Tools, Equipment for Work	X		X	P D L
Animals	X		X	P D L
Fields and Flocks	X			P D L
Seeds at Planting Time	X		X	P D L
Occasion of Thanksgiving for Harvest	X			P D L
Athletic Event	X			P D L
Before /After Meals [4 plans, seasons]	X			P D L

BLESSINGS OF OBJECTS THAT ARE DESIGNED OR ERECTED FOR USE IN CHURCHES EITHER IN THE LITURGY OR IN POPULAR DEVOTIONS				
Blessing of	**Outside Mass**	**Within Mass**	**Shorter Rite**	**Proper Minister**
Baptistry or New Baptismal Font	X			B P [D]
With Celebration of Baptism	X			
Without Celebration of Baptism	X			
Repository for Holy Oils	W	X	X	P D
Episcopal or Presidential Chair	W	X		B P
Lectern (Ambo)	W	X		B P
Tabernacle	X			B P
Confessional (outside or within Penance Service)	X	Never		B P
New Church Doors	X			B P
New Cross for Public Veneration	X			B P
Image of Our Lord Jesus Christ	X	Never		B P
Image of the BVM	X	Never		B P
Image of the Saints	X	Never		B P
Bells	X			B P
Organ	X			B P
Articles for Liturgical Use	X	X	X	B P [D]
Chalice and Paten	W	X		B P
Holy Water outside Mass	X			B P
Stations of the Cross	X			B P
Cemetery	X			B P

BLESSINGS OF ARTICLES MEANT TO FOSTER DEVOTION OF THE CHRISTIAN PEOPLE				
Blessing of	**Outside Mass**	**Within Mass**	**Shorter Rite**	**Proper Minister**
Religious Articles	X		X	P D
Rosaries	X		X	P D
Blessing & Conferral of Scapular	X			Inst.

BLESSINGS RELATED TO FEAST AND SEASONS				
Blessing of	**Outside Mass**	**Within Mass**	**Shorter Rite**	**Proper Minister**
Advent Wreath	W	X	X	P D Parents
Christmas Manger/Nativity Scene	W	X	X	P D L
Christmas Tree	X		X	P D L
Homes—Christmas and Easter Seasons	X		X	P D L
Throats—Feast of St. Blaise (Feb. 3)	W	X	X	P D L
Blessing and Distribution of Ashes	X			P D [L]
St. Joseph's Table (March 19)	X		X	P D L
Blessing of Food for First Meal of Easter	X		X	P D L
Mother on Mother's Day	X		X	P
Father on Father's Day	X			P
Visiting a Cemetery on All Soul's Day, Memorial Day, or Anniversary of Death or Burial	X			P D L
Blessing of Food for Thanksgiving Day	W	X	X	P D L
Food/Drink/Other for Devotions	X	Feast		P D

BLESSINGS FOR VARIOUS NEEDS AND OCCASIONS				
Blessing of	**Outside Mass**	**Within Mass**	**Shorter Rite**	**Proper Minister**
Those Who Exercise Pastoral Service	W	X		P D
Readers	W	X		Pastor P D
Altar Servers, Sacristans, Musicians, Ushers	W	X		Pastor P D
Commissioning of Extraordinary Ministers of Holy Communion	W	X		Pastor P D
Parish Council	W	X		Pastor P D
Officers of Parish Societies	X			Pastor P D
Welcoming of New Parishioners	X			Pastor
Departing Parishioner	X			Pastor
Those Receiving Ecclesiastical Honors	X			Bishop
On Occasion of Inauguration of a Public Official	X			P D L
Blessing in Thanksgiving	X			P D L
Blessing to be Used in Various Circumstances	X			P D L

APPENDICES				
Blessing of	**Outside Mass**	**Within Mass**	**Shorter Rite**	**Proper Minister**
Installation of a Pastor				
When a Bishop Presides		X		B
When a Priest Presides		X		P
Solemn Blessings *May conclude any blessing in Book of Blessings, Morning or Evening Prayer, or any occasion when a bishop, priest, or deacon presides (see Sacramentary).*	X	X		B P D
Prayers over the People— General, on Feasts of Saints *(same)*	X	X		B P D

Pastoral Care of the Sick

> Is there anyone sick among you? Let him send for the presbyters of the Church and let them pray over him, anointing him with oil in the name of the Lord. The prayer of faith will save the sick man and the Lord will raise him up. If he has committed any sins, they will be forgiven him (James 5:14-15).

On November 30, 1972, Pope Paul VI promulgated an apostolic constitution entitled *Sacram Unctionem Infirmorum* and promulgated the *editio typica* of *Ordo Unctionis Infirmorum eorumque pastoralis curae (The Rite of Anointing and Pastoral Care of the Sick)*. The USA translation (1974) was entitled simply *Pastoral Care of the Sick*. This new rite better reflected the true, public nature of the Church's ministry to the sick.

Three major changes may be noted from previous rites: First, the rite was placed in the broader context of pastoral care, not treated as an isolated ritual of the Church. Second, human sickness was no longer linked to human sinfulness, but immersed in the mystery of salvation; human suffering was joined to the suffering of Christ. Third, the rite now contained much more than formulae for priests. It included Scripture, gestures, the use of oil, and a variety of liturgical roles.

No longer called *extreme unction*, the sacrament was made more available to those who were chronically ill, facing major surgery, or fighting debilitating diseases as well as those in the end stages of terminal illnesses.

Look carefully at the outlines that follow. Note the distinction between the rites for the sick and the rites for the dying. Note when oil is used and when it is not. See if you can find the situation(s) when several sacraments are utilized—penance, Eucharist (viaticum), the anointing of the sick, and even confirmation.

General Introduction (1–41)

Part I: Pastoral Care of the Sick

    I. Visits to the Sick (54–61)
        Introduction (42–53)
        Visits to the Sick (54–61)
        Introduction
        Reading
        Response
        The Lord's Prayer
        Concluding Prayer
        Blessing

    II. Visits to a Sick Child (62–70)
        Introduction
        Reading
        Response
        The Lord's Prayer
        Concluding Prayer
        Blessing

    III. Communion to the Sick (71–96)
        Introduction (71–80)
        Communion in Ordinary Circumstances (81–91)
            Introductory Rites
            Liturgy of the Word
            Liturgy of Holy Communion
            Concluding Rite
        Communion in a Hospital or Institution (92–96)
            Introductory Rite
            Liturgy of Holy Communion
            Concluding Rite

    IV. Anointing of the Sick (97–160)
        Introduction (97–110)
        Anointing outside Mass (111–130)
            Introduction

Order of Christian Funerals

At the time of a death, the Church is called to a ministry of consolation—to pray for the dead and to comfort those who mourn (OCF 8). In addition, the funeral and related rites offer an opportunity to instruct the faithful about the paschal character of death.

> By means of the funeral rites it has been the practice of the Church . . . not simply to commend the dead to God but also to raise high the hope of its children and to give witness to its own faith in the future resurrection of the baptized with Christ (Decree, OCF, 8-15-69).

The revised rites reflect the ancient idea of "stations" or praying at various locales in a progressive format. In the *Order of Christian Funerals,* you will find a service for gathering in the presence of the body, for the reception of the body at the church, for a Scripture-based vigil service, a funeral liturgy within or outside of Mass, and prayers for the committal of the body.

Part II recognizes the special pastoral needs of a family and community that must bury a child. A vigil, funeral liturgies, and rite of committal are provided.

Parts III and IV include a wealth of alternative prayers and readings, including an Office for the Dead for Morning and Evening Prayer.

When cremation must take place before the funeral liturgy, the presider may turn to a recent appendix to the OCF. It was approved by the US bishops in November 1996, confirmed by Rome in July 1997, and its use made mandatory in the USA on November 2, 1997. OCF 411–431 elucidates on a funeral in the presence of cremated remains. Articles 432–438 provide optional texts for such an occasion.

General Introduction (1–49)

Part I: Funeral Rites

Vigil and Related Rites and Prayers
    Vigil for the Deceased (54–81)
        Introductory Rites
        Liturgy of the Word
        Prayer of Intercession
        Concluding Rite
    Vigil for the Deceased with Reception at the Church (82–97)
        Introductory Rites
        Liturgy of the Word
        Prayer of Intercession
        Concluding Rite

Holy Communion and Worship of the Eucharist outside Mass

Congregation for Divine Worship and the Discipline of the Sacraments

The eucharistic sacrifice is the source and culmination of the whole of Christian life. Therefore, our eucharistic liturgies, particularly on Sundays, should be prepared with utmost care and celebrated with reverence and joy. Since her beginning, the Church has gathered to hear the Word of God, to offer thanks to him, and to share in the eucharistic banquet. This was Christ's command.

The Church also has a rich tradition of sharing Communion and worshiping the Eucharist outside of Mass. We learn from Justin Martyr that Communion was brought to those who were absent from the assembly (*First Apology,* ca. 150). Until the practice was stopped, pilgrims would take consecrated bread home and consume it on weekdays. In the Middle Ages, architectural elements, the Latin language, theological controversies, and even changes in the liturgy itself convinced the faithful that they might be too unworthy to participate in the Mass fully or to receive Communion frequently. They developed public and private rituals for adoring the Blessed Sacrament, either reserved in a tabernacle or exposed in a monstrance. The Church codified (and limited the use of) some of these practices and created rites for their proper celebration.

In 1973, the CDWDS promulgated *Holy Communion and Worship of the Eucharist outside Mass.* Some antecedents for HCWEOM may be found in the *Roman Ritual of 1614* and in its regular revisions by later popes (1752, 1884, 1925, 1952, and 1960). HCWEOM contains official liturgies (and important *praenotanda*) for pastoral situations where Holy Communion is distributed apart from the Mass, including "Communion services" (Chapter I) and Communion to the sick and the dying (Chapter II). Its third chapter provides guidelines for the adoration and exposition of the Blessed Sacrament, eucharistic congresses, and eucharistic processions.

Both ordinary and extraordinary ministers of Holy Communion may use these rites, but note carefully those times when alternative prayers are provided for lay ministers. These rites provide additional opportunities, outside Mass, to become more aware of Christ's presence in his Church and to be in spiritual communion with him.

General Introduction (1–12)

Chapter I: Holy Communion outside Mass (13–53)

Introduction

The Relationship between Communion outside Mass and
the Sacrifice
The Time of Communion outside Mass
The Minister of Communion
The Place of Communion outside Mass
Regulations for Giving Communion
Dispositions for Communion

Rite of Distributing Communion outside Mass (26–53)

The Long Rite with the Celebration of the Word (26–41)
Introductory Rites
Celebration of the Word of God
Holy Communion
Concluding Rite
The Short Rite with the Celebration of the Word (42–53)
Introductory Rites
The Short Form of the Reading of the Word
Holy Communion
Concluding Rite

*Chapter II: Administration of Communion and Viaticum to the Sick
by an Extraordinary Minister (54–78)*

The Ordinary Rite of Communion to the Sick (56–63)

Introductory Rite
The Short Form of the Reading of the Word
Holy Communion
Concluding Rite

The Short Rite of Communion to the Sick (64–67)

Viaticum (68–78)

Introductory Rite
The Short Form of the Reading of the Word
Profession of Baptismal Faith
Prayer for the Sick Person
Viaticum
Concluding Rite

Order for the Solemn Exposition of the Holy Eucharist

This book was developed by the USCCB as a supplement to Chapter III of *Holy Communion and Worship of the Eucharist outside Mass*. It encourages the occasional exposition of the Eucharist and offers a collection of rites and texts for use during a period of solemn exposition.

Quoting heavily from HCWEOM, the Introduction provides an excellent explanation of the relationship between Mass and exposition.

> Exposition of the holy eucharist, either in the ciborium or in a monstrance, leads us to acknowledge Christ's marvelous presence in the sacrament and invites us to the spiritual union with him that culminates in sacramental communion. Therefore it is a strong encouragement toward the worship owed to Christ in spirit and truth.
>
> In such exposition care must be taken that everything clearly brings out the meaning of eucharistic worship in its correlation with the Mass. There must be nothing about the appointments used for exposition that could in any way obscure Christ's intention of instituting the eucharist above all to be near us to feed, to heal, and to comfort us.
>
> During the exposition of the blessed sacrament, celebration of the Mass in the body of the church or oratory is prohibited (OSEHE 7–8).

Quoting heavily from HCWEOM, the book reviews liturgical laws and proper procedures for the exposition of the Blessed Sacrament. It then provides a wide variety of liturgical celebrations, readings, prayers, and music suggestions for use during the period of exposition. One should note that devotions and exercises of popular piety are not among the offerings.

Introduction

History (1–2)
Mystery of the Eucharist (3–6)
Relationship between Exposition and Mass (7–8)
Signs of Reverence to the Blessed Sacrament (9–10)
Solemn Exposition (11–14)
Adoration (15)
Liturgy of the Hours and Exposition (16)
Eucharistic Processions (17–25)
Minister of Exposition (26)
Vesture (27)

Chapter I: Opening Celebration of the Eucharist (28–36)

Rite of Blessing of Oils, Rite of Consecrating the Chrism

This rite, used by the bishop during the Chrism Mass at your cathedral during Holy Week, can be prayed during various parts of the Mass as shown, or all three oils may be blessed/consecrated after the priests' Renewal of Commitment (See the Appendix II of the Sacramentary).

Introduction (1–12)

Blessing of the Oils and Consecration of the Chrism (13–28)

Preparations

> Liturgy of the Word
> Renewal of Priestly Commitment

Rite of Blessing

> Procession with the Oils and the Gifts
> Hymn
> Presentation of the Oils and the Gifts

Liturgy of the Eucharist

> Preparation of the Altar and the Gifts
> Eucharistic Prayer
> Blessing of the Oil of the Sick (20)
> Communion Rite

Blessing of the Oil of Catechumens (21–22)

Consecration of the Chrism (23–26)

Concluding Rite

These oils, then, are distributed to the parishes of the diocese. At the Evening Mass of the Lord's Supper on Holy Thursday, these oils may be presented to the parish community.

LITURGY OF THE HOURS

In his first letter to the Thessalonians, Paul exhorted his Church to "pray unceasingly" (1 Thess 5:17). The Church has always taken these words seriously. Recognizing that all time is God's, we consecrate the year, seasons, weeks, days, and even hours to him. Building on Jewish traditions, the exercise of this ceaseless prayer has taken various forms over the centuries. The praxis of the early Church, monastic and religious communities, and urban churches influenced its structure and content. But psalms and other Scripture passages have always been the foundation of these prayers of praise and supplication.

Vatican II called for the revision of the breviary of Pius V (cf. SC, Chapter VI). This not only meant a revision of the breviary or *Divine Office,* but a renewed appreciation that this important liturgy of the Church was indeed meant to be prayed by all the faithful.

"Pastors should see to it that the chief hours, especially vespers, are celebrated in common in church on Sundays and the more solemn feasts . . . " (SC 100).

The *General Instruction of the Liturgy of the Hours* [GILH] was released on February 2, 1971. The *editio typica* of the revised *Liturgy of the Hours* was released a few months later on April 11, 1971. In general, it promoted the "hinge hours" of Morning and Evening Prayer, offered several forms of Midday Prayer, simplified Night Prayer, and compiled an Office of Readings (OOR)—Scripture and excerpts from spiritual writers. The psalms were distributed over a four-week cycle in such a way that few psalms were eliminated. Some psalms, traditionally assigned to Morning Prayer and Evening Prayer, were utilized more frequently, as well as psalms most appropriate to the Hour.

Sometimes the Liturgy of the Hours is published in Four Volumes—Advent and Christmas Season; Lenten Season and Easter Season; Ordinary Time, Weeks 1–17; and Ordinary Time, Weeks 18–34. A condensed version, entitled *Christian Prayer* is also available in one volume.

Elsewhere in this book, you will find more detailed information on the GILH. In the Appendix, you will find planning sheets for Morning Prayer, Evening Prayer, and Night Prayer. In addition, the Appendix contains easy-to-follow charts listing the psalms and canticles of the four-week cycles.

Introductions

Apostolic Constitution

General Instruction of the Liturgy of the Hours

Table of Liturgical Days

Principle Celebrations of the Liturgical Year

General Roman Calendar

Proper of the Seasons [varies by volume]

    Advent Season
        Before December 16
        After December 16
    Christmas Season
        Before the Epiphany
        After the Epiphany
    Lenten Season
        Before Holy Week
        Holy Week
        Easter Triduum
    Easter Season
        Before Ascension
        After Ascension
    Sundays in Ordinary Time
    Solemnities

The Ordinary of the Liturgy of the Hours

Psalter

    Week I
    Week II
    Week III
    Week IV
    Night Prayer

    Complementary Psalmody

Proper of Saints (January to December)

Commons

> Dedication of a Church
> Blessed Virgin Mary
> Apostles
> Martyrs (several, one)
> Pastors
> Doctors of the Church
> Virgins
> Holy Men and Women

Offices for the Dead

Appendices

> Canticles and Gospel Readings for Vigils
> Shorter Forms of Intercessions to Be Used at Evening Prayer
> Additional Prayers for Use at the Liturgy of the Hours
> Poetry
> Proper for the United States

Indices

> Index of Psalms
> Index of Canticles
> Index of Biblical Readings
> Index of Nonbiblical Readings
> Index of Hymns
> Alphabetical Index of Celebrations

ROMAN PONTIFICAL

In 1978, ICEL published an English translation of the Roman Pontifical. Actually, the content of the book corresponded to *Pars Prima* (the first part) of the *Pontificale Romanum* of 1596, issued by Clement VIII in accord with a decree of the Council of Trent. Those rites had been revised by decree of the Second Vatican Council and published in Latin by the authority of Pope Paul VI during the period from 1968 to 1972. ICEL's translations were approved by various conferences of bishops in their respective territories and these, in turn, were confirmed by the Apostolic See in the years that followed (1974–78).

The 1978 publication contained rites for the Enrollment of Names, Christian Initiation, Confirmation, and Reception into Full Communion with the Catholic Church; the Institution of Readers and Acolytes; the Ordination of Deacons, Priests, and Bishops; the Blessing of Persons; and other liturgical texts.

Later that same year, the ICEL translation of the *Rite of Dedication of a Church and an Altar* was approved for use in the dioceses of the USA and confirmed by the Congregation for the Sacraments and Divine Worship (9-25-78). A revised edition was published in 1989.

The Rite(s) of Ordination were further revised by Pope John Paul II. The vernacular edition was approved by the USCCB on November 12, 2002, and subsequently confirmed by the Apostolic See on February 4, 2003.

The rites in the Roman Pontifical are used by a bishop or the superior of an order, but parish liturgists should be familiar with their contents.

Rite of Dedication of a Church and an Altar

If your parish is involved in building a new worship space or renovating an existing one, you will certainly want to study this rite. Indeed, the texts can serve as a wonderful source for reflection during the development phase of the project.

Each chapter of the rite addresses a specific scenario and each chapter comes with its own thorough introduction. Turn to chapter I when blessing the construction site or laying a foundation stone. Chapter II is used for the dedication of a new church and altar; indeed the church should not be used until it is dedicated with this rite. Chapter III is used when churches have undergone some renovation. Chapter IV provides *praenotanda* and texts for the dedication of a new altar. Use chapter V when blessing a chapel or an oratory and chapter VI for the blessing of an altar. Chapter VII contains an order of blessing for a chalice and paten (see also *Book of Blessings*). Finally, the appendix provides a special text for the *Litany of the Saints* on the occasion of the dedication of a church.

Chapter I: Laying of a Foundation Stone or Commencement of Work on the Building of a Church

Introduction (1–8)
Rite of Blessing (9–31)
    Approach to the Construction Site (two forms)
    Reading of the Word of God
    Blessing of the Site of the New Church
    [Blessing and Laying of the Foundation Stone]
    Concluding Rite

Chapter II: Dedication of a Church

Introduction (1–27)
Rite of Dedication
    Introductory Rites (28–52)

Rite of Confirmation

See pages 58–59.

Rite of Ordination

Ordination is one sacrament conferred in several degrees. "The divinely established ecclesiastical ministry is exercised at different levels by those who from antiquity have been called bishops, presbyters, and deacons" (Decree of Promulgation, Paul VI). The rite used to confer this sacrament was also revised by postconciliar commissions and on June 18, 1968, Pope Paul VI approved a new Rite of Ordination. Its use became effective on Easter Sunday, April 6, 1969.

The rite was further revised by Pope John Paul II. This second typical edition was promulgated on June 29, 1989. ICEL produced an English translation in 1999 and the USCCB approved it on November 13, 2002. The Apostolic See confirmed it on December 4, 2002, and its use became mandatory in the dioceses of the USA on June 29, 2003.

The second typical edition *(editio typica altera)* now begins with the *Rite of Ordination of a Bishop.* This simple editorial change emphasizes three things—(1) that the bishop has the fullness of the sacrament of holy orders; (2) that priests are coworkers with the bishop; and (3) that deacons are ordained to serve his ministry (Decree of Promulgation).

In the Prayer of Ordination for priests and deacons, the words required for the validity of the sacrament remain unchanged, but phrases drawn from the New Testament were added—a reminder that these orders derive from Christ the High Priest. The Promises of the Elect (formerly the Examination) have been slightly rearranged. New questions have been added for priests, more specific to the ministry of reconciliation and the celebration of the Eucharist. The ordination of deacons includes a rite of commitment to celibacy, waived when the rite is used for the ordination of permanent deacons. New titles appear such as "Litany of Supplication" and "Explanatory Rites." The "Rite of Admission to Candidacy for Holy Orders" is now placed in the appendix.

The rite of episcopal ordination stands as tribute to apostolic succession and the special role of bishop as teacher, shepherd, and high priest of his flock. For example, the Prayer of Ordination is based on an ancient consecratory prayer found in the *Apostolic Tradition* (ca. 215). It follows the Laying on of Hands and the Presentation of the Book of the Gospels.

De Ordinatione Episcopi, Presbyterorum et Diaconorum, editio typica altera

Rite of Ordination of a Bishop, of Priests, and of Deacons, second typical edition

Decree—June 29, 1989

Decree—August 15, 1968

Apostolic Constitution

General Introduction

> Sacred Ordination (1–6)
> The Structure of the Celebration (7–10)
> Adaptations for Different Regions and Circumstances (11)

Chapter I: Ordination of a Bishop

> Introduction

>> The Importance of Ordination (12–14)
>> Duties and Ministries (15–18)
>> The Celebration of Ordination (19–27)
>> Requisites for the Celebration (28–30)

> Rite of Ordination of a Bishop (31–64)
> Rite of Ordination of Several Bishops (65–100)

Chapter II: Ordination of Priests

> Introduction

>> The Importance of Ordination (101–102)
>> Duties and Ministries (103–106)
>> The Celebration of Ordination (107–114)
>> Preparation for the Celebration (115–117)

> Rite of Ordination of Priests (118–144)
> Rite of Ordination of a Priest (145–172)

Chapter III: Ordination of Deacons

> Introduction

>> The Importance of Ordination (173–178)
>> Duties and Ministries (179–180)

Other Rites in the Pontifical

Institution of Ministers and the Blessing of Persons

Chapter I: Institution of Readers

Introduction (1)
Liturgy of the Word (2)
Institution of Readers (3–7)
    Calling of the Candidates
    Homily
    Invitation to Prayer
    Prayer
    Institution [presentation of Scriptures]
Liturgy of the Eucharist (8)

Chapter II: Institution of Acolytes

Introduction (1)
Liturgy of the Word (2)
Institution of Acolytes (3–7)
    Calling of the Candidates
    Homily
    Invitation to Prayer
    Prayer
    Institution
Liturgy of the Eucharist (8)

Chapter III: Biblical Readings

Blessing of Persons (incorporated into the Book of Blessings)

Order for the Blessing of Persons Who Exercise Pastoral Service

Introduction (1808–1810)
Order of Blessing within Mass (1811–1813)
Order of Blessing within a Celebration of the Word of God (1814–1826)

Order for the Blessing of Readers

Introduction (1827–1830)
Order of Blessing within Mass (1831–1833)
Order of Blessing within a Celebration of the Word of God (1834–1846)

Order for the Blessing of Altar Servers, Sacristans, Musicians, and Ushers

Introduction (1847–1851)
Order of Blessing within Mass (1832–1854)
Order of Blessing within a Celebration of the Word of God (1855–1870)

Order for the Commissioning of Extraordinary Ministers of Holy Communion

Introduction (1871–1873)
Order of Commissioning within Mass (1874–1881)
Order of Commissioning within a Celebration of the Word of God (1882–1896)

Consecration to a Life of Virginity

Consecration to a Life of Virginity (1–10)
Consecration to a Life of Virginity for Women Living in the World (1–38)
Consecration to a Life of Virginity Together with Religious Profession for Nuns (39–80)
Appendix

Rite of Religious Profession

Part I: Rite of Religious Profession for Men

I. Introduction (1–15)
    Norms for the Rite of Initiation into the Religious Life (1–13)
II. Rite of Temporary Profession during Mass (14–39)
III. Rite of Perpetual Profession during Mass (40–77)
IV. Rite of Renewal of Vows during Mass (78–90)
V. Other Texts for the Rites of Religious Profession

Part II: Rite of Religious Profession for Women

I. Introduction (1–13)
II. Rite of Temporary Profession during Mass (14–42)
III. Rite of Perpetual Profession during Mass (43–84)
IV. Rite for Renewal of Vows during Mass (85–97)
V. Other Texts for the Rites of Religious Profession

Blessing of Abbotts or Abbesses

I. Blessing of an Abbott (1–32)
II. Blessing of an Abbess (1–22)

Blessing of Objects and Places

> Rite of Blessing of Oils, Rite of Consecrating the Chrism (incorporated into BB, Sacramentary, Appendix II)

Blessing of Papal Insignia

Order of Crowning an Image of the Blessed Virgin Mary
(This rite is to be used by a bishop or a priest.)

> Introduction (1–12)
>
> Chapter I: Crowning of an Image of the BVM within Mass (13–20)
>
> Chapter II: Crowning of an Image of the BVM within Evening Prayer (21–31)
>
> Chapter III: Crowning of an Image of the BVM within a Celebration of the Word of God (32–43)

SUNDAY CELEBRATIONS IN THE ABSENCE OF A PRIEST (USA)

On June 2, 1988, the Congregation for Divine Worship published a *Directory for Sunday Celebrations in the Absence of a Priest*. It reiterated the Church's teaching on the meaning of Sunday, indicated the conditions under which celebrations in the absence of a priest may legitimately take place, and provided guidelines for executing such celebrations. Since it was the responsibility of the conference of bishops to prepare more detailed norms and to produce a ritual adapted to the culture and needs of their people, the NCCB produced the ritual *Sunday Celebrations in the Absence of a Priest (SCAP)* that could be used by deacons and laypeople. It became effective on January 1, 1994, and may be used in dioceses where the local bishop has authorized its use. The continued use of this document in the USA is currently under discussion by the USCCB.

The introduction recalls the importance of Sunday in the life of the Church; discusses the priest shortage (6–9); outlines the conditions for using SCAP (10–13); defines the role of the bishop, priest, and deacon; describes the forms the Sunday celebration may take—Morning or Evening Prayer or a Liturgy of the Word (25–26)—then goes into detail regarding individual parts of the liturgy (37–49). It concludes with notes regarding preparation for the celebration.

One must be careful not to confuse SCAP with *The Rite of Distributing Holy Communion outside Mass* [see above, *Roman Ritual*, HCWEOM]. Carefully review the outline of SCAP below and note the differences.

Introduction

Chapter I: Morning and Evening Prayer with Holy Communion

Morning Prayer

> Introductory Rites
>> Introduction
>> Hymn
>
> Psalmody
>> Antiphon I
>> Psalm
>> [Psalm Prayer]
>> Antiphon 2
>> Old Testament Canticle
>> Antiphon 3
>> Psalm
>> [Psalm Prayer]

Liturgy of the Word
    First Reading
    Responsorial Psalm
    Second Reading
    Gospel Acclamation
    Gospel
    Homily or Reflection on the Readings
    Response to the Word of God (Responsory)
    [Dismissal of the Catechumens]
    Canticle of Zechariah
    Intercessions

	OR	Communion Rite
Lord's Prayer		Lord's Prayer
		Sign of Peace
		Invitation to Communion
		Communion
Concluding Prayer		Prayer after Communion

Concluding Rite
    Brief Announcements
    [Collection of Monetary Offerings of the Assembly]
    Blessing
    Dismissal

Evening Prayer

Introductory Rites
    Introduction
    Hymn

Psalmody
    Antiphon I
    Psalm
    [Psalm Prayer]
    Antiphon 2
    Psalm
    [Psalm Prayer]
    Antiphon 3
    New Testament Canticle

Liturgy of the Word
    First Reading
    Responsorial Psalm
    Second Reading

Gospel Acclamation
Gospel
Homily or Reflection on the Readings
Response to the Word of God (Responsory)
[Dismissal of the Catechumens]
Canticle of Zechariah
Intercessions

	OR	Communion Rite
Lord's Prayer		Lord's Prayer
		Sign of Peace
		Invitation to Communion
		Communion
Concluding Prayer		Prayer after Communion

Concluding Rite
Brief Announcements
[Collection of Monetary Offerings of the Assembly]
Blessing
Dismissal

Chapter II: Celebration of the Liturgy of the Word [with Holy Communion]

Introductory Rites
Greeting
Introduction
Litany of Praise of God's Mercy
Opening Prayer

Liturgy of the Word
First Reading
Responsorial Psalm
Second Reading
Gospel Acclamation
Gospel
Homily or Reflection on the Readings
[Dismissal of the Catechumens]
Profession of Faith
General Intercessions
Act of Thanksgiving

	OR	Communion Rite
Lord's Prayer		Lord's Prayer
		Sign of Peace

Invitation to Communion
Communion
Concluding Prayer   Prayer after Communion

Concluding Rite
Brief Announcements
[Collection of Monetary Offerings of the Assembly]
Blessing
Dismissal

Appendices—Additional Texts

I. General Intercessions

II. Acts of Thanksgiving

III. Prayers of the Day and Prayers after Communion—Sundays, Solemnities, Feasts

IV. Additional Prayers after Communion

V. Blessings

VI. Directory for Sunday Celebrations in the Absence of a Priest (CDW)
Preface (1–7)
Sunday and Its Observance (8–17)
Conditions for Holding Sunday Celebrations in the Absence of a Priest (18–34)
Order of Celebration (35–50)

FOR FURTHER READING

Austin, Gerald. *Anointing with the Spirit: The Rite of Confirmation, The Use of Oil and Chrism.* New York: Pueblo Publishing Company, 1985.

Bradshaw, Paul. *Daily Prayer in the Early Church.* London: SPCK and New York: Oxford, 1982.

———. *Two Ways of Praying.* Nashville: Abingdon Press, 1995.

Coffey, David. *The Sacrament of Reconciliation. Lex Orandi* Series. Collegeville: The Liturgical Press, 2002.

Glen, Genevieve. *Recovering the Riches of Anointing: A Study of the Sacrament of the Sick.* Collegeville: The Liturgical Press, 2002.

Johnson, Maxwell. *The Rites of Initiation: Their Evolution and Interpretation.* Collegeville: The Liturgical Press, 1999.

———, ed. *Living Water, Sealing Spirit: Readings on Christian Initiation.* Collegeville: The Liturgical Press, 1995.

Kavanagh, Aidan. *Confirmation: Origins and Reform.* New York: Pueblo Publishing Company, 1988.

———. "Confirmation: A Suggestion from Structure," in Maxwell E. Johnson, ed., *Living Water, Sealing Spirit: Readings on Christian Initiation.* Collegeville: The Liturgical Press, 1995, 148–158.

———. *The Shape of Baptism: The Rite of Christian Initiation.* New York: Pueblo Publishing Company, 1978.

Lewinski, Ron. *Guide for Sponsors.* Archdiocese of Chicago: Liturgy Training Publications, 1980. Spanish version by Pedro Rodriguez, CMF.

McMahon, J. Michael. *Seek the Living God: Bulletin Inserts Regarding the RCIA.* Washington, D.C.: Federation of Diocesan Liturgical Commissions, 1990.

Milne, Mary. *Sunday Dismissals for the RCIA.* Collegeville: The Liturgical Press, 1993.

Mitchell, Nathan. *Cult and Controversy.* New York: Pueblo Publishing Company, 1982.

Murphy Center for Liturgical Research. *Made, Not Born: New Perspectives on Christian Initiation and the Catechumenate.* Notre Dame, Ind.: University of Notre Dame Press, 1976.

Searle, Mark. *Christening: The Making of Christians.* (Especially Part Three.) Collegeville: The Liturgical Press, 1980.

Secretariat of the Bishops' Committee on the Liturgy. *Ceremonial of Bishops: A Reader— Proceedings of the National Workshop on the Ceremonial of Bishops,* 1989. Washington, D.C.: United States Catholic Conference, 1994.

Sieverding, Dale. *The Reception of Baptized Christians: A History and Evaluation.* Forum Essay #7. Archdiocese of Chicago: Liturgy Training Publications, 2002.

Simons, Thomas. *Holy People, Holy Place: Rites for the Church's House.* Archdiocese of Chicago: Liturgy Training Publications, 1998.

Taft, Robert. *The Liturgy of the Hours in East and West: The Origins of the Divine Office and Its Meaning for Today.* Second revised edition. Collegeville: The Liturgical Press, 1993.

Turner, Paul. "The Origins of Confirmation: An Analysis of Aidan Kavanagh's Hypothesis," (with response from Kavanagh) in Maxwell Johnson, ed., *Living Water, Sealing Spirit: Readings on Christian Initiation.* Collegeville: The Liturgical Press, 1995, 238–258.

———. *Ages of Initiation: The First Two Christian Millennia.* Collegeville: The Liturgical Press, 1999.

Yarnold, Edward. *The Awe-Inspiring Rites of Initiation: The Origins of the RCIA.* Collegeville: The Liturgical Press, 1994.

Ritual Texts

Leccionario I, II, y III

The Rites of the Catholic Church, Volumes I and II. New York: Pueblo, 1983.

Rito de la Iniciacion Cristiana de Adultos

Rito del Matrimonio

Ritual de las Exequias Cristianas—Misa Funeral, Vigilia

Chapter IV

Documents That Accompany
the Liturgical Books

⌘

General Instruction of the Roman Missal (2002)

Adaptations to the General Instruction of the Roman Missal
for the Dioceses of the United States (2002)

Introduction to the Order of Mass:
A Pastoral Resource of the BCL (2003)

General Norms for the Liturgical Year and the Calendar (1969)

Introduction to the Book of the Gospels (2000)

Lectionary for Mass: An Introduction (1969, 1981, 1999)

Norms for the Distribution and Reception of Communion under Both
Kinds for the Dioceses of the United States of America (April 17, 2002)

Book of Blessings: General Introduction (1989)

Ceremonial of Bishops (1989)

General Instruction of the Liturgy of the Hours (February 2, 1971)

Directory for Sunday Celebrations
in the Absence of a Priest (June 2, 1988)

⌘

The liturgical books and their *praenotandae* contain essential information, theological principles, and juridic norms for the preparation and celebration of parish liturgies. In addition, one will find valuable information in various guidelines, instructions, and pastoral letters. It is highly recommended that Parish Worship Commissions and others who prepare liturgies should be familiar with these resources.

Please be aware that not all documents are of the same nature nor bear the same canonical authority or weight.

> The documents pertaining to the universal Latin-rite Roman Catholic Church are of three kinds: a conciliar constitution, liturgical law from select liturgical books, and a directory from a Roman congregation. The documents pertaining to the churches in the United States are of two kinds: norms approved by the [USCCB], which are binding in all dioceses of the United States, and documents published by the [USCCB] committees that serve as pastoral directives for the benefit of all persons interested in good worship (John Huels, "General Introduction" to *The Liturgy Documents: A Parish Resource*, Volume I. Archdiocese of Chicago: Liturgy Training Publications, 1991, ix–xiv).

THE CANONICAL WEIGHT OR LEVEL OF AUTHORITY OF A DOCUMENT (HUELS)

1) A Conciliar Constitution
2) Liturgical laws from select liturgical books
3) Directory from a Roman Congregation
4) Norms approved by the USCCB binding on all dioceses in the United States
5) Documents published by USCCB committees which serve as pastoral directives. They are not optional. These are not strictly liturgical law, but are based on documents that are. They can become diocesan policy if a bishop so decrees.

On the following pages, you will find a select list of liturgical documents. An outline and brief summary of each document is supplied.

GENERAL INSTRUCTION OF THE ROMAN MISSAL

Pope John Paul II, Congregation for Divine Worship and Discipline of the Sacraments

All liturgical books begin with *praenotanda,* i.e., introductions which offer theological principles and juridic norms for proper celebration. The Roman Missal is no exception. This is appropriately called the *General Instruction* since it gives directives for *how* things are to be done as well as explanations for *why.* Since the Roman Missal was revised by Pope John Paul II in 2000, the GIRM which accompanied it was revised as well. The *Institutio Generalis Missalis Romani* was printed within the *Missale Romanum, editio typica tertia* when it was published in March 2002. The decree of promulgation states that it takes effect on the Solemnity of the Body and Blood of the Lord—June 25, 2000. The English translation was confirmed on March 17, 2003.

The GIRM begins with an expanded treatise on the theology of our eucharistic celebrations, then explains the basic structure and parts of the Mass. Since the Constitution on the Sacred Liturgy called for a restoration of a variety of ministries and roles at Mass, the liturgical reforms promoted them. Chapter III describes these ministries and the duties assigned to each.

Chapter IV examines various pastoral circumstances. It provides instructions for Masses in which there is a congregation, at which only one minister participates, at which a deacon is present or absent, directions for concelebrated Masses, and, finally, general norms for all Masses.

Chapter V addresses the arrangement and furnishing of churches, giving some latitude to the local bishop to establish regulations within his diocese. Chapter VI describes, in finer detail, regulations on the requisites for Mass, including vessels, vestments, and other furnishings.

Chapters VII and VIII are invaluable reading for those who prepare liturgies since they outline principles for the choice of Mass and its parts, including directives for Masses for Various Circumstances and Masses for the Dead.

Chapter IX, an all-new addition, lists those things that are the purview of the local bishop or the conference of bishops to adapt or change as well as those items that are reserved to the Apostolic See.

ADAPTATIONS TO THE GENERAL INSTRUCTION OF THE ROMAN MISSAL FOR THE DIOCESES OF THE UNITED STATES OF AMERICA

On November 14, 2001, the Latin Rite bishops of the USCCB approved adaptations to the GIRM as particular law for the dioceses of the United States. Chapter IX of the GIRM specifically recommends such adaptation so that the liturgical celebrations may reflect the pastoral and cultural realities of a diverse Church. These adaptations were confirmed by the CDWDS on April 17, 2002, and became effective in the dioceses of the USA on March 25 of that year.

Formerly, such adaptations were found in a "United States Appendix to the General Instruction." Now they will be incorporated into the actual text directly into the relevant paragraph. For example, GIRM 154 states that at the Kiss of Peace the priest "always remains in the sanctuary, so as not to disturb the celebration." But the USCCB inserted a sentence which reads, "In the dioceses of the United States of America, for a good reason, on special occasions, (for example in the case of a funeral, a wedding, or when civic leaders are present) the priest may offer the sign of peace to a few of the faithful near the sanctuary."

Other adaptations for the dioceses of the USA include:

43.2   The faithful may sit or kneel during the period of religious silence after Communion.

43.3   The faithful kneel during that portion of the Eucharistic Prayer that follows the Sanctus until after the Great Amen, except when prevented on occasion by reason of health, lack of space, the large number of people present, or some other good reason. Those who do not kneel should make a profound bow when the priest genuflects after the consecration.

48   four options for the *Cantus ad introitum*

61.4   options for the responsorial psalm

87   four options for the *Cantus ad Communionem*

154.2   The priest may leave the sanctuary to offer the sign of peace to a few of the faithful on special occasions such as a funeral or wedding.

160.2   posture and gesture for the faithful during the reception of Holy Communion

283.3   In all that pertains to Communion under both kinds, the *Norms for the Distribution and Reception of Holy Communion Under Both Kinds in the Dioceses of the USA* are to be followed.

301   Material for a sacred altar may be wood provided that the altar is structurally immobile.

304   Uppermost cloth on the altar is white.

326   materials for sacred furnishings

329   materials for sacred vessels

339   vesture or suitable clothing for lay ministers

346   color of sacred vestments

362   Readings for Mass; adaptations contained in the Lectionary for Mass for the Dioceses of the USA should be carefully observed.

373   Special days of prayer as designated by the diocesan bishop; January 22 (or 23rd when the 22nd falls on a Sunday) shall be observed as a particular day of penance for violations to the dignity of human persons committed through acts of abortion; Mass for Peace and Justice should be used.

393   Musical settings of the texts for the people's responses and acclamations in the Order of Mass and special rites must be submitted to the USCCB for review and approval prior to publication; organ is accorded pride of place but other instruments may be used if "they are truly apt for sacred use or can be rendered apt."

INTRODUCTION TO THE ORDER OF MASS: A PASTORAL RESOURCE OF THE BISHOPS' COMMITTEE ON THE LITURGY

The *Introduction to the Order of Mass* was designed to assist those who prepare liturgical celebrations as well as those who are responsible for the formation of liturgical ministers and the faithful. It is an official commentary on the universal law of the Church as articulated in the *General Instruction of the Roman Missal*. In 1997, ICEL described the purpose of the *Introduction to the Order of Mass:* (1) to clarify and systematize material in the GIRM by bringing together varying treatments of the same subject; (2) to supplement the GIRM with relevant material from other rites and documents; (3) to promote the observance of the directives found in the GIRM by offering further pastoral reasoning; (4) to provide explanations for adaptations made by the conference of bishops; (5) to support the idea of various roles within the liturgy; and (6) to offer reasons for choices of texts and offer suggestions for more effective celebrations, including weekdays (ICEL, 1997 *Progress Report* as summarized by Msgr. Anthony Sherman in "A New Resource: The Pastoral Introduction to the Order of Mass," *Pastoral Music*, June–July 2003).

The document has undergone an extensive review process in light of the changes introduced to the *Order of Mass* in the *Institutio Generalis Missalis Romani* in 2000 and 2002. In July of 2000, the Congregation noted that it did not have any objections to the publication of the document, made some changes, but suggested that the document be printed separately from the Missal (ibid.).

In June 2002 the Bishops' Committee on the Liturgy (USCCB) incorporated into the IOM recently approved and confirmed U.S. adaptations to the GIRM (Introduction, p. xiii) as well as the *Norms for the Distribution and Reception of Holy Communion . . .* (Sherman, *Pastoral Music*).

The document was published in booklet form in July 2003.

I. The Celebration of Mass

    Liturgical Ministers and the Gathered Assembly
        Priest Celebrant
        Deacon
        Lector
        Gathered Assembly
        Liturgical Musicians
        Extraordinary Ministers of Holy Communion
        Servers
        Ushers

The Eucharistic Celebration and Its Symbols
    Gesture and Posture
        Posture
        Other Postures and Gestures
    Words
        Sacred Scripture
        Presidential Prayers
        Common Prayers and Other Texts
        Sung Texts
        Invitations and Introductions
        Private Prayers
    Liturgical Music
    Silence
    Materials and Objects
        Bread and Wine
        Sacred Vessels
        Altar
        Ambo
        Chair
        Cross
        Books
        Vesture
        Incense
Adapting the Celebration to Particular Circumstances

II. Introductory Rites

    Entrance Procession
        Greeting
        Act of Penance
        Rite of Blessing and Sprinkling of Water
        Gloria
        Opening Prayer (Collect)

III. Liturgy of the Word

    Biblical Readings

    Responsorial Psalm

    Gospel Acclamation

    Sequence

    Gospel Reading

    Homily

Profession of Faith (Creed)

Prayer of the Faithful (Universal Prayer)

IV. Liturgy of the Eucharist

Preparation of the Gifts
    Preparation of the Altar
    Presentation of the Gifts
    Placing of the Gifts on the Altar
    Mixing of Wine and Water
    Incense
    Washing of Hands
    Prayer over the Offerings

Eucharistic Prayer
    Dialogue
    Preface
    Sanctus Acclamation
    Epiclesis
    Institution Narrative and Consecration
    Memorial Acclamation
    Anamnesis and Offering
    Intercessions
    Doxology

Communion Rite
    The Lord's Prayer
    Sign of Peace
    Breaking of the Bread
    Communion
        Private Preparation of the Priest
        Invitation to Holy Communion
        Distribution of Holy Communion
        Communion Song
        Purification of Sacred Vessels
        Period of Silence or Song of Praise
    Prayer after Communion

V. Concluding Rite

Announcements
Greeting
Blessing
Dismissal

GENERAL NORMS FOR THE LITURGICAL YEAR
AND THE CALENDAR

It is vitally important that those who prepare parish liturgies understand how the Church year is ordered since "through the yearly cycle the Church unfolds the entire mystery of Christ and keeps the anniversaries of the saints" (GNLYC 1) and since "each day is made holy through the liturgical celebrations of the people of God, especially through the eucharistic sacrifice and divine office" (3). The *General Norms for the Liturgical Year and the Calendar* is the source for such knowledge. You'll find it in the front of your Sacramentary.

GNLYC begins by explaining the theology and arrangement of the various days, beginning with Sunday, the weekly celebration of the Lord's Resurrection. Next, it explains the rank assigned to particular days—solemnity, feast, obligatory memorial, or optional memorial.

The Easter Triduum is the "culmination of the entire liturgical year." Paragraphs 18–21 elucidate the Triduum's importance. Next, the document elaborates on the seasons of Easter, Lent, Christmas, Advent, and Ordinary Time—explaining the calculation of their days and the facets of the paschal mystery which they call to mind. On rogation and ember days, the Church prays for particular needs and gives public thanks to God.

The first part of chapter two explains the General Calendar and addresses how religious communities and diocesan and regional Churches may prepare and insert particular calendars with the approval of the Apostolic See. Next, the document gives instructions for entering proper dates, e.g., that the celebration of a saint is usually assigned to the date of his or her death. In 1969, the calendar was simplified and revised. It now includes in its sanctoral cycle modern saints—both lay and religious—and honors saints from every continent.

You will want to refer often to the "Table of Liturgical Days According to Their Order of Precedence" (59). The first days listed, of course, are the days of the Easter Triduum—they have priority over any other liturgical celebration. When choosing among Mass texts and readings for liturgical days which may coincide, it will be important to know each day's rank and order of precedence.

I. The Liturgical Year

    Liturgical Days (3–16)
        The Liturgical Day in General
        Sunday
        Solemnities, Feasts, and Memorials
        Weekdays

INTRODUCTION TO THE BOOK OF THE GOSPELS

While the *Introduction to the Lectionary for Mass* certainly has salient references to the gospel reading, the *Introduction to the Book of the Gospels* offers important theological and rubrical notes specific to the gospel and to the use of the *Book of the Gospels*. It quotes heavily from other documents, including *The Introduction to the Lectionary for Mass,* the *General Instruction of the Roman Missal,* the *Ceremonial of Bishops,* the Constitution on the Sacred Liturgy, and from Scripture.

The first four paragraphs remind us that the "Church received the Gospel from the Apostles to whom the Lord explained the Holy Scriptures" (2) and the central role the gospel plays in the Church's liturgy and life. Next, the IBG recalls the history of the *Book of the Gospels* itself and its use in liturgical rites and ecclesial ceremonies.

Part II gives specific instructions for the proper use of the *Book of the Gospels* at Mass. It details its proper use in the entrance procession (9); provides considerations for the preparation of the gospel procession (10–12); elaborates on the blessing of the deacon by the priest (13); and offers alternative procedures in the absence of a deacon (14–15). It describes the gospel procession (16); the proclamation of the gospel (17–19); and the acclamation at the end of the gospel (20–21). Finally, it notes that the *Book of the Gospels* is never carried out in the procession at the end of Mass (22).

I. The Centrality of the Gospel in the Life of the Church and Her Liturgy (1–7)

II. The Proclamation of the Gospel at Mass (8–22)

LECTIONARY FOR MASS: AN INTRODUCTION

When the latest edition of the *Lectionary for Mass* was approved (1997), it provided the occasion to compose an expanded introduction. The new text first "gives a general statement of the essential bond between the word of God and the liturgical celebration"(1), then deals in greater detail with the word of God at Mass and the structure of the Order of Readings. It is an invaluable resource for all ministers of the Word who want to understand the nature of the Lectionary, for those who prepare liturgies, and for lectors who wish to reflect on their role in proclaiming the Word of God to the assembly. Indeed, chapter I may be an ideal foundation for an evening of reflection with your parish lectors.

Chapter II describes the Liturgy of the Word at Mass and its parts. Chapter III discusses the various offices and ministries in the Liturgy of the Word—the presider, the faithful, and the reader.

"Throughout the liturgical year . . . the choice and sequence of readings are aimed at giving Christ's faithful an ever-deepening perception of the faith they profess and of the history of salvation"(60). Therefore, chapter IV reviews the Order of Readings and the reasons behind their selection and arrangement.

Chapter V describes the Order of Readings in detail, beginning with Advent and progressing through the liturgical year.

Conferences of bishops are charged with providing translations of the Lectionary for their territories, so chapter VI lists norms regarding translation, format, style, and other adaptations that the bishops must consider.

Preamble

Chapter I. General Principles for the Liturgical Celebration of the Word of God

Certain Preliminaries (1–3)

a) The Importance of the Word of God in Liturgical Celebration
b) Terms Used to Refer to the Word of God
c) The Significance of the Word of God in the Liturgy

Liturgical Celebration and the Word of God (4–6)

a) The Proper Character of the Word of God in the Liturgical Celebration
b) The Word of God in the Economy of Salvation
c) The Word of God in the Liturgical Participation of the Faithful

The Word of God in the Life of the People of the Covenant (7–10)

a) The Word of God in the Life of the Church
b) The Church's Explanation of the Word of God
c) The Connection between the Word of God Proclaimed and the Working of the Holy Spirit
d) The Essential Bond between the Word of God and the Mystery of the Eucharist

First Part: The Word of God in the Celebration of the Mass

Chapter II. The Celebration of the Liturgy of the Word at Mass

The Elements of the Liturgy of the Word and Their Rites (11–31)

a) The Biblical Readings
b) The Responsorial Psalm
c) The Acclamation before the Reading of the Gospel
d) The Homily
e) Silence
f) The Profession of Faith
g) The Universal Prayer or Prayer of the Faithful

Aids to the Proper Celebration of the Liturgy of the Word (32–37)

a) The Place for the Proclamation of the Word of God
b) The Books for Proclamation of the Word of God in the Liturgy

NORMS FOR THE DISTRIBUTION AND RECEPTION
OF HOLY COMMUNION UNDER BOTH KINDS
FOR THE DIOCESES OF THE UNITED STATES OF AMERICA

In chapter 9 of the GIRM, the text elaborates on the adaptations which were the purview of the conference of bishops (390) and the diocesan bishop (387). Among the duties of the conference is to establish norms for the manner of receiving Holy Communion (cf. GIRM 160, 238, 387).

On June 15, 2001, the Latin Rite bishops of the USCCB approved a directory entitled *Norms for the Distribution and Reception of Holy Communion Under Both Kinds for the Dioceses of the United States of America* (hereafter *Norms*). This replaced an earlier directory entitled *This Holy and Living Sacrifice*. Like all directories, *Norms* drew from a wide variety of sources, including the GIRM itself, the Sacramentary, *Eucharisticum Mysterium: On the Worship of the Eucharist (1967)*, *Immensae Caritas*, and others.

Norms was confirmed by the CDWDS on March 22, 2002, and became particular law for the dioceses of the USA on April 7, 2002.

Part I of the *Norms* consists of an extended reflection on the mystery of the Eucharist and the theological foundation for distributing and receiving Holy Communion under both species. Part II turns to more ecclesial, pastoral, and practical matters in order to ensure the proper, reverent, and, careful distribution of Holy Communion under both kinds. Here, the bishops address when Holy Communion may be given under both kinds, the need for proper catechesis on this practice, and the role of the diocesan bishop in establishing local policies. Rightfully, the bishops stress reverence for the sacrament at all times.

BOOK OF BLESSINGS: GENERAL INTRODUCTION

Congregation for Divine Worship

In 1989, the USCCB promulgated a USA edition of the *Book of Blessings,* an interim collection of blessings containing the Roman *De Benedictionibus* and forty-two original blessings composed by the BCL. All thirty-nine articles of the *General Introduction* deserve close reading as do the introductory paragraphs which precede each blessing. Nearly one-fifth of the book is commentary and these paragraphs provide rich fodder for theological reflection in addition to pastoral applications.

The first part of the BBGI recalls the role of blessings in salvation history encased in wonderful trinitarian theology. The second part reviews "Blessings in the Life of the Church" stressing that they have their foundation in the word of God and their motives in faith. Like all liturgy, blessings "are directed toward human sanctification and God's glorification . . . prepare us to receive the chief effect of the sacraments, and make holy the various situations of human life" (14).

Part three addresses the offices and ministries proper to blessings, emphasizing that communal celebration is always desirable and often obligatory. Even when objects are "blessed," the Church is really invoking God's blessing on those who will use them.

A bishop may preside at any of the blessings found in the *Book of Blessings;* indeed, some are restricted to him. Priests, deacons, instituted acolytes and readers, laymen and laywomen may also preside, depending on the nature and occasion of the blessing. The proper minister is stipulated before each Order of Blessing.

One who prepares these liturgies will want to pay particular attention to part four. Therein, BBGI outlines the typical structure of the rite (20–24) and lists the signs to be used (26a-e). The manner of joining a blessing to other liturgical celebrations (28–30), the guidelines for preparations (31–34), and notes regarding vesture (35–38) are treated concisely.

Finally, the BBGI concludes with permission for each conference of bishops to adapt the ritual to the needs of their region.

CEREMONIAL OF BISHOPS

The *Ordines Romani* of the seventh century recorded the norms for liturgical services celebrated by the pope. After a long line of development, Clement VIII issued a *Caeremoniale Episcoporum* in 1600. At least four editions were published in the centuries that followed. Since Vatican II called for the reform of the rites, the *Ceremonial of Bishops* also needed to be revised. On September 7, 1984, Pope John Paul II approved and ordered the publication of a new *Ceremonial of Bishops.*

The *Ceremonial of Bishops* is not a liturgical book in the proper sense, since it is not a text used for liturgical celebrations. Rather, it describes the rites typically celebrated by a bishop and is a helpful resource for bishops, masters of ceremonies, other ministers, and diocesan offices of worship. It collects pastoral and juridic norms from the various liturgical books that directly pertain to a bishop and adds more provisions "with the intention of achieving a liturgy . . . that is genuine, simple, clear, dignified, and pastorally effective" (Decree of Promulgation, CDW, 9-14-84). Liturgies at which the bishop presides stand as a model for all other celebrations since they are the "principal manifestation of the particular Church" (Preface CB, cf. SC 41).

Part I: General Considerations

Part II: Mass

> Stational Mass of the Diocesan Bishop
> Other Masses Celebrated by the Bishop
> Mass at Which the Bishop Presides but Not as Celebrant

Part III: Liturgy of the Hours and Celebrations of the Word of God

Part IV: Celebrations of the Mysteries of the Lord through the Cycle of the Liturgical Year

Part V: Sacraments

Part VI: Sacramentals

Part VII: Special Days in the Life of a Bishop

Part VIII: Liturgical Celebrations in Connection with Official Acts Pertaining to the Government of a Diocese

Appendices

GENERAL INSTRUCTION OF THE LITURGY OF THE HOURS

Congregation for Divine Worship

The *General Instruction of the Liturgy of the Hours* [GILH] was released on February 2, 1971. The *editio typica* of the revised *Liturgy of the Hours* soon followed on April 11, 1971. In general, it promoted the "hinge Hours" of Morning and Evening Prayer, several forms of daytime prayer, vigils, and a simplified Night Prayer. It also compiled an Office of Readings (OOR)— a collection of Scripture passages and excerpts from spiritual writers. The psalms were distributed over a four-week cycle in such a way that few psalms were eliminated. Some psalms, traditionally assigned to Morning Prayer and Evening Prayer, were utilized more frequently, as well as psalms most appropriate to the Hour.

While the document itself is filled with tensions and apparent contradictions, it is worthy of a full reading, especially its first chapter on the theology of the Hours (nos. 1–19). The following paragraphs give you just a glimpse:

> The purpose of the liturgy of the hours is to sanctify the day and the whole range of human activity. Therefore, its structure has been revised in such a way as to make each hour correspond as nearly as possible and to take account of the circumstances of life today. . . . It is best that each of them be prayed at a time most closely corresponding to the true canonical hour (GILH 11).

> To the different hours of the day the liturgy of the hours extends the praise and thanksgiving, the memorial of the mysteries of salvation, the petition and the heavenly glory that are present in the eucharistic mystery, the center and high point of the whole Christian community (GILH 12).

> . . . Those taking part in the liturgy of the hours have access to holiness of the richest kind through the life-giving word of God, which in this liturgy receives great emphasis. Thus its readings are drawn from sacred Scripture, God's words in the psalms are sung in his presence, and the intercessions, prayers, and hymns are inspired by Scripture and steeped in its spirit (GILH 14).

Chapter I: Importance of the Liturgy of the Hours in the Life of the Church

Prayer of Christ (3–4)
Prayer of the Church (5–9)
Liturgy of the Hours (10–19)
Participants in the Liturgy of the Hours (20–33)

DIRECTORY FOR SUNDAY CELEBRATIONS IN THE ABSENCE OF A PRIEST

Congregation for Divine Worship

The decree from the Congregation for Divine Worship which promulgated this directory acknowledged that it was not always and everywhere possible for Catholic communities to celebrate the Eucharist on Sunday. So after broad consultation, it offered this directory "to guide and prescribe what should be done when real circumstances require the decision to have Sunday celebrations in the absence of a priest."

The first part of the directory summarizes the meaning of Sunday. The second part prescribes the conditions necessary for the decision in a diocese to schedule, as a regular occurrence, Sunday assemblies in the absence of a priest. The third part describes a rite for Sunday Celebrations of the Word along with the distribution of Communion.

"The fundamental point of the entire directory is to ensure, in the best way possible and in every situation, the Christian celebration of Sunday."

Preface (1–7)

Chapter I. Sunday and Its Observance (8–17)

Chapter II. Conditions for Holding Sunday Celebrations in the Absence of a Priest (18–34)

Chapter III. Order of Celebration (35–50)

Chapter V

Other Liturgical Documents and Pastoral Letters

⌘

Sacrosanctum Concilium:
Constitution on the Sacred Liturgy (December 4, 1963)

Built of Living Stones (USCCB, November 16, 2000)

Comme le Prévoit: On the Translation of Liturgical Texts
for Celebrations with a Congregation (January 25, 1969)

Criteria for the Evaluation of Inclusive Language Translations
of Scriptural Texts Proposed for Liturgical Uses
(NCCB, November 15, 1990)

Dies Domini: On Keeping the Lord's Day Holy (May 31, 1998)

Directory for Masses with Children (1973)

Directory for the Application and Norms on Ecumenism (June 8, 1993)

Ecclesia de Eucharistia (April 17, 2003)

Fulfilled in Your Hearing: The Homily in the Sunday Assembly (1982)

Gather Faithfully Together (1997)

God's Mercy Endures Forever: Guidelines on the Presentation
of Jews and Judaism in Catholic Preaching (NCCB, 1988)

Guidelines for the Celebration of Sacraments
with Persons with Disabilities (NCCB, 1995)

Inculturation and the Roman Liturgy:
Fourth Instruction for the Right Application
of the Conciliar Constitution on the Liturgy, nos. 37–40 (1994)

Liturgiam Authenticam: Fifth Instruction on the Right Application
of the Conciliar Constitution on the Liturgy (CDWDS, 2001)

Liturgical Music Today (1982)

Music in Catholic Worship (1972, 1983)

Paschale Solemnitatis: Circular Letter on Preparing
and Celebrating the Paschal Feasts (1988)

Plenty Good Room: The Spirit and Truth of
African American Catholic Worship (NCCB , 1990)

To Speak as a Christian Community:
Pastoral Message on Inclusive Language (August 16, 1989)

⌘

SACROSANCTUM CONCILIUM:
CONSTITUTION ON THE SACRED LITURGY

Vatican II

It is said that a late Supreme Court Justice always carried a miniature edition of the US Constitution in his pocket. Likewise, anyone who prepares liturgies should keep this gem of a document at their fingertips, consulting it frequently.

The *Constitution on the Sacred Liturgy* echoes earlier Church documents and is the result of nearly a century of liturgical research and renewal. Since the reform of the liturgy reformed the Church, the council sought to revise the rites "carefully in the light of sound tradition . . . that they be given new vigor to meet the circumstances and needs of modern times" (4).

Sacrosanctum Concilium offered, first, general principles for the reform of the liturgy and began with a firm foundation in liturgical theology (1–10). Then it outlined procedures for the reform of each rite. It placed high priority on the full, conscious, and active participation of the people and regularly referred to the need for catechesis on the liturgy (11, 14, 48, 63, 113). Toward that end, SC called for the reform of each rite of the Church, mandating that such reform be characterized by "noble simplicity" (34) and that text be rendered in the vernacular (36). So that the "genius and talents of various races and peoples" might be respected and fostered, SC championed the creative, but faithful adaptation of the Roman Rite (37–40). It stressed repeatedly the role of the conferences of bishops, local bishops, priests, and seminaries in promoting the liturgical life of the faithful.

Chapter II concentrates on the eucharistic liturgy, especially the Order of the Mass and the promotion of Sacred Scripture.

Chapter III elaborates on the other sacraments and sacramentals. Chapter IV calls for the reform of the Divine Office asking that "the traditional sequence of the hours . . . be restored so that once again they be genuinely related to the hour of the day. . . ." (88). Recognizing that in the cycle of a year, "the Church unfolds the whole mystery of Christ" (102), chapter V elaborates on each liturgical season and emphasizes the primacy of Sunday. Chapters VI and VII address sacred music, sacred art and furnishings, and their impact on the full, conscious, and active participation of the people. A brief Appendix notes that the council was "not opposed" to considering a fixed day for Easter nor a perpetual calendar.

The Constitution on the Sacred Liturgy lays the foundation for our understanding of the very nature of liturgy. Read it in its entirety before you read any other liturgical document or book. No summary attempted here can do it justice.

Introduction (1–4)

Chapter I: General Principles for the Reform and Promotion of the Sacred Liturgy (5–46)

I. Nature of the Liturgy and Its Importance in the Church's Life (5–13)
II. Promotion of Liturgical Instruction and Active Participation (14–20)
III. The Reform of the Sacred Liturgy (21–40)
    A. General Norms
    B. Norms Drawn from the Hierarchic and Communal Nature of
        the Liturgy
    C. Norms Based on the Teaching and Pastoral Character of the
        Liturgy
    D. Norms for Adapting the Liturgy to the Culture and Traditions
        of Peoples
IV. Promotion of Liturgical Life in Diocese and Parish (41–42)
V. Promotion of Pastoral-Liturgical Action (43–46)

Chapter II: The Most Sacred Mystery of the Eucharist (47–58)

Chapter III: The Other Sacraments and Sacramentals (59–82)

Chapter IV: Divine Office (83–101)

Chapter V: The Liturgical Year (102–111)

Chapter VI: Sacred Music (112–121)

Chapter VII: Sacred Art and Sacred Furnishings (122–130)

Appendix: Declaration of the Second Vatican Ecumenical Council on the Revision of the Calendar

BUILT OF LIVING STONES

Promulgated by the bishops of the United States, this document replaces *Environment and Art in Catholic Worship* (BCL, 1978).

Recognizing that the building in which the Church worships expresses and fosters faith and affects worship, *Built of Living Stones* draws on universal legislation. It serves as a resource for dioceses as they develop local guidelines on the building and renovation of churches.

The first chapter offers a theology of the Church as a "temple built of living stones" and urges that the building which houses this Church must "reflect and inspire the prayer of the community" (18). BLS then offers basic principles for building or renovating churches—the design must (1) be in harmony with Church laws and serve the needs of the liturgy, (2) foster participation in the liturgy, (3) reflect the various roles of the participants, and (4) respect the culture of every time and place.

Chapter II stresses that the building must be suited for the celebration of the Eucharist and the other rites of the Church. It carefully elaborates on each area of the church and furnishings therein, then addresses the requirements of various rites and specific days of the liturgical year. Finally, it speaks of the use and placement of sacred images and materials related to devotions.

Citing a dynamic tension between traditional artistic expression and art which "articulates the faith proper to each age and culture" (141), the third chapter discusses the "marriage between faith and art" and how worthy art is marked with "quality and appropriateness" (146–149).

The final chapter addresses practical considerations in the building process. These include the development of a master plan; dialogue between the diocese and the parish; assessment and self-study; hiring professionals, e.g., the liturgical design consultant, architect, and contractors; the design of the church and its surroundings; and special issues in the renovation of churches.

COMME LE PRÉVOIT: ON THE TRANSLATION OF LITURGICAL TEXTS FOR CELEBRATIONS WITH A CONGREGATION

Consilium

   The Constitution on the Sacred Liturgy articulated the objectives and goals of the liturgical reform. A committee called the Consilium (1964–1969) and the Congregation for Divine Worship (1969–) were charged with the task of carrying them out. Since the most important goal was the "full, conscious, and active participation of the people" (SC 11, 14), the production of texts in the "mother tongue" of the people was imperative. Through a series of letters, directives, and speeches by Pope Paul VI, and this document, the Consilium established criteria and procedures for the translation of texts into the vernacular. The text itself was a model of collaboration, drafted in six languages.

   The first part offers general principles for translation. The document notes that a liturgical text is, as a ritual sign, a means of communication. Its purpose is no less than "to proclaim the mystery of salvation" (6). " . . . It is not sufficient that a liturgical translation merely reproduce the expressions and ideas of the original text. Rather it must faithfully communicate to a given people, in their own language, that which the Church . . . intended to communicate to another people in another time" (ibid.).

   Several techniques should be employed—the best available critical or original text, a sense of the unity of meaning, a recognition of literary form, an acknowledgment of the ritual act being performed, and an understanding of the full context of the passage. The resultant words must be accessible to the people, yet worthy of the mystery being celebrated (15). This approach is known as "dynamic equivalence" in contrast to a word-for-word translation.

"The prayer of the Church is always the prayer of some actual assembly here and now. It is not sufficient that a formula handed down from some other time or region be translated verbatim . . . " (20). So, *Comme le Prévoit* advocated not only a faithful translation from the Latin, but the revision of texts in light of pastoral experience as well as the creation of new texts.

Part II addresses the translation of particular liturgical texts (both sung and spoken) and characteristics of speech. It cautions against paraphrasing biblical texts or the Roman liturgy, particularly eucharistic and other sacramental formulas. It suggested that liturgical texts be produced in collaboration with other Christians with whom we share a common heritage.

The last part establishes guidelines and methodology for those committees who will be responsible for producing translations, including those "mixed commissions," e.g., International Committee for English in the Liturgy, Inc. (ICEL), which serve several conferences of bishops with a shared language (41–42). Finally, CP recognizes that new texts will be necessary but "any new forms adopted should in some way grow organically from forms already in existence" (CP 43; SC 23).

Introduction (1–4)

I. General Principles (5–29)

II. Some Particular Considerations (30–37)

III. Committees for Translating

CRITERIA FOR THE EVALUATION OF INCLUSIVE LANGUAGE TRANSLATIONS OF SCRIPTURAL TEXTS PROPOSED FOR LITURGICAL USE

It is the responsibility of conferences of bishops to provide translations of the liturgical books (cf. SC 36; CP 2; IO 40; CIC 825.1). So in 1990, the bishops of the United States established a set of principles before beginning a new translation of the *Lectionary for Mass*. They recognized five historical developments that would impact their work—(1) the introduction of the vernacular; (2) the sensitivity to exclusive language in American culture; (3) the loss of grammatical gender; (4) other changes in English vocabulary— words once generic that had become gender specific; and (5) the increased tendency of some pastoral leaders to provide impromptu, ill-informed changes to liturgical texts.

Primarily, two guiding principles governed their work—(1) fidelity to the Word of God and (2) the full, conscious, and active participation of the assembly.

In Part II of CEIL, the bishops focused on the issue of inclusive language itself. Since by its very nature the word of God is inclusive (14) the bishops developed principles for Lectionary translations—(1) reflect on the original cultural context of the passage; (2) inclusive language in public communication has evolved—avoid words once considered generic which are now gender specific; (3) avoid language which denies the dignity of all the baptized; and (4) maintain the gender of individual persons in scriptural narratives and parables.

The third part of CEIL addresses issues for the preparation of texts to be used in the Lectionary, including the need for exegetical and linguistic review, an appreciation of cultural and liturgical contexts, and the addition of *incipits* and transitional phrases which would improve audibility. The psalms have a long tradition of such adaptation for liturgical use.

Part IV turns to specific questions of "horizontal" and "vertical" language. In the naming of God, the translator will use a masculine pronoun or repeat the word "God." In the naming of Christ, one must preserve his male humanity to complement the christological meanings of Old Testament passages. In the naming of the Trinity, the titles of "Father," "Son," and "Holy Spirit" or masculine pronouns are to be employed. In naming the Church, the third person neuter may be used instead of various titles (e.g., the Body of Christ) unless its antecedents use male or female imagery (e.g., the Bride of Christ).

The translation of the Lectionary, then, became subject to this set of original criteria and other rules. Later, *Liturgiam Authenticam* guided the work of the translators. The first volume of the revised translation of the *Lectionary for Mass* appeared in 1999.

Introduction: Origins and Nature of the Problem (1–6)

I. General Principles (7–13)

> Fidelity to the Word of God
> The Nature of the Liturgical Assembly

II. Principles for Inclusive Language Lectionary Translations (14–20)

III. Preparation of Texts for Use in the Lectionary (21–24)

IV. Special Questions (25–31)

> a) Naming God in Biblical Translations
> b) Naming Christ in Biblical Translations
> c) Naming the Trinity in Biblical Translations
> d) Naming the Church in Biblical Translations

Conclusion

DIES DOMINI: ON KEEPING THE LORD'S DAY HOLY

Pope John Paul II

If your parish worship commission is ever looking for a retreat instrument, this is it! With rich imagery and abundant quotations from Scripture, Pope John Paul II invites us to experience anew the fullness of the paschal mystery on each Sunday, "The Lord's Day."

> It is Easter which returns week by week, celebrating Christ's victory over sin and death, the fulfillment in him of the first creation and the dawn of "the new creation" (2 Cor 5:17). It is the day which recalls in grateful adoration the world's first day and looks forward in active hope to "the last day when Christ will come in glory" (Acts 1:11; 1 Thess 4:13-17) and all things will be made new (Rev 21:5) (DD 1).

If we better understood the different facets of the day, he contends, we would better understand our duty and privilege to keep Sunday holy (7).

So the Pope reintroduces us to the richness of Sunday in all its facets, utilizing the various titles given to Sunday to do so. In chapter I, he links the resurrection of Christ, the New Creation, with the work of the Creator. Just as God sanctified the seventh day, the Sabbath, and prescribed a day of rest, God gave us Jesus, the new Sabbath, and made possible eternal rest.

In chapter II, Pope John Paul II concentrates on *Dies Christi* and "the intimate bond between Sunday and the resurrection of the Lord" (19). He invites you to meditate on more titles and their christological implications—the First Day of the Week, the Day of New Creation, the Eighth Day, the Day of Light, the Day of the Spirit, etc.

Focusing on *Dies Ecclesiae* (the *Day of the Church*) he places special emphasis on the Sunday assembly—where Christians gather at the tables of the Word and the Eucharist "to experience and proclaim the presence of the Risen Lord and are called to evangelize and bear witness in their daily lives" (45). Since Eucharist is the very heart of Sunday, "the pastors of the church have never ceased to remind the faithful to take part in the liturgical assembly" (46). Here, titles for Sunday include the Day of the Church and the Day of Hope. Finally, the Pope addresses pastoral realities of assemblies without a priest and communion with the homebound.

In chapter IV, *Dies Hominis*, he describes Sunday as a day of joy, rest, and solidarity. "Sunday is a day of joy in a special way, indeed the day most suitable for learning how to rejoice and to rediscover the true nature and deep roots of joy—the joy of the risen Christ, the perfect image and revelation of humanity as God intended" (57, 58). This day of rest brings solidarity, especially through the Eucharist.

Christ is the Alpha and Omega of time (74) and on Sunday, we celebrate the primordial feast, revealing the meaning of all time. In chapter V, *Dies Dierum*, the Pope analyzes the whole of the liturgical year, indeed all of time, in light of the paschal mystery of Jesus Christ. Finally, the Pope reminds all Christians that on Sunday they are called to celebrate their salvation and the salvation of all humanity (82).

This is one document that cannot be easily synthesized. Every person and every assembly should meditate on each paragraph and resolve to "keep holy the Lord's Day."

DIRECTORY FOR MASSES WITH CHILDREN

Congregation for Divine Worship

Like all "directories," the *Directory for Masses with Children* provides "directions." In this case, it offers principles for the adaptation of the liturgy for children so that they may participate in the Eucharist more fully and "gradually open their minds to the perception of Christian values and the celebration of the mystery of Christ" (DMC 9).

The Introduction traces the history of the document's development and notes that DMC is concerned with the needs of children who have not yet reached adolescence.

Chapter I addresses ways to introduce the liturgy to children. It stresses the importance of the family and the faith community in the catechesis and liturgical participation of children.

Chapter II briefly speaks of the Sunday assembly and suggests ways to foster young parishioners' attention and participation.

The final chapter offers principles for the adaptation of [weekday] Masses with children at which only a few adults are present. The children's participation in song and in various ministries is encouraged, with the realization that eucharistic Communion is the highpoint of participation in the Mass. While some rituals and texts may never be changed and the integrity of the eucharistic prayer must be maintained, the priest is allowed free use of commentary. He may also reduce the number of readings. The document concludes with suggestions for (and specific limitations on) adapting various parts of the Mass.

Since the publication of DMC, the *Lectionary for Masses with Children* and three eucharistic prayers for children have been published; these, too, carefully adapt the readings and our great prayer(s) of thanksgiving in ways suited to children.

Introduction (1–7)

I. The Introduction of Children to the Eucharistic Celebration (8–15)

II. Masses with Adults in Which Children Also Participate (16–19)

III. Masses with Children in Which Only a Few Adults Participate (20–54)

> Offices and Ministries in the Celebration (22–24)
> Place and Time of Celebration (25–28)
> Preparation for the Celebration (29)
> Singing and Music (30–32)

Gestures (33–34)
Visual Elements (35–36)
Silence (37)
Parts of the Mass (38–54)

DIRECTORY FOR THE APPLICATION AND NORMS ON ECUMENISM

Pontifical Council for Promoting Christian Unity

Reiterating the Church's commitment to ecumenical endeavors and to realizing the vision of Christian unity, the Pontifical Christian Unity Council issued this directory in 1993. It revises and expands documents issued in 1967 and 1970 and "brings together all the norms already established for implementing and developing the decisions of the council . . . " (6).

DAPNE offers a full exploration of the reasons for and the means by which unity must be pursued, but liturgists will want to pay attention to particular passages. Article 62 states that "since liturgy is the primary and indispensable source from which the faithful are to derive the Christian Spirit" (SC 14), Catholics should (1) participate in the celebration of the Eucharist to be drawn into unity with God and with each other and (2) foster prayer among Christians particularly during the Week of Prayer for Christian Unity (January 18–25) and the days between Ascension and Pentecost.

Chapter IV is devoted to "Communion in Life and Spiritual Activities." After a thorough discussion on baptism, the authors cover such topics as prayer offered in common, liturgical worship, and the shared use of sacred space. Those who plan ecumenical services will want to note the structure and guidelines elucidated in Article 111. Both nonsacramental prayer (116–121) and the sacramental life (122–137) are cautiously discussed, including the role of Catholic ministers in the administration of the sacraments under special circumstances. Other pastoral situations, including schools, hospitals, and mixed marriages, are addressed.

"Veneration of the Scriptures is a fundamental bond of unity between Christians . . . " (183). Therefore, DAPNE advocates common biblical study and common witness to the saving Word. Finally, ecclesial communities might call upon their shared, ancient heritage to prepare common liturgical texts, hymnals, and orders of readings (187).

In ecumenism, too, it is apparent that liturgy serves as source and summit to all the Church's activities.

ECCLESIA DE EUCHARISTIA

John Paul II

"The Church draws her life from the Eucharist." With this simple, but profound statement, Pope John Paul II begins a beautiful encyclical letter on the mystery of the Eucharist and how the sacrament relates to the Church. Appropriately, it was signed on Holy Thursday, 2003, during the Mass of the Lord's Supper.

Recalling the words of the Constitution on the Sacred Liturgy, the Pope reminds us that the Eucharistic sacrifice is the "source and summit of the Christian life" (SC 10). "The Church was born of the paschal mystery . . . and two thousand years later . . . we continue to relive that primordial image of the Church. At every celebration of the Eucharist, we are spiritually brought back to the paschal Triduum" (3). With this encyclical, he wanted "to rekindle this Eucharistic amazement" (6).

In the first chapter he explains the sacrificial nature of the Eucharist, wherein "the body given up" and "the blood poured out" by Christ is sacramentally made present at each celebration—the one sacrifice of the Cross (12). The gift of Christ's love and obedience to the Father is a gift given for our sake (13). He further reflects on the reality of transubstantiation (15) and the saving efficacy of receiving the Lord in Holy Communion (16). He preaches on the eschatological dimensions of the sacrament and its implications for social justice (20).

In the second chapter, he stresses that the fruit of the Eucharist is unity. The Church is united to her Lord and the members with one another as the Body of Christ (23). The Eucharist builds the Church and the Church makes the Eucharist. As another sign of Christ's abiding presence in his Church, the worship of the Eucharist outside of Mass should be linked to the Eucharistic sacrifice and encouraged by pastors (25).

In the third chapter, the Pope reflects on the role of the bishop and the priest and their role as servant for the sake of the community. Again, we receive the Eucharist as a gift at their hands.

The Eucharist is not only a means of communion, it presupposes communion and strengthens it; it creates it and builds it. In this context, we must be committed to ecumenism.

In the fifth chapter he addresses the dignity of the eucharistic celebration and the joy which must be present as the assembly gathers around the Lord. He stresses that we need to recover a sense of dignity and beauty in our celebrations and in every art form which we employ.

The sixth chapter focuses on Mary, "Woman of the Eucharist," who became the first tabernacle. Her *Magnificat* must resound in the heart of all believers.

Finally, the Pope challenges us to pursue a path to holiness, not through some new program, but through the sacrament of the Eucharist. In it, Christ himself is to be known, loved, imitated, and proclaimed.

Introduction

The Mystery of Faith

The Eucharist Builds the Church

The Apostolicity of the Eucharist and the Church

The Eucharist and Ecclesial Communion

The Dignity of the Eucharistic Celebration

At the School of Mary, Woman of the Eucharist

Conclusion

FULFILLED IN YOUR HEARING:
THE HOMILY IN THE SUNDAY ASSEMBLY

Bishops' Committee on Priestly Life and Ministry

This document addresses "the intimate link between preaching and the celebration of the sacraments" and why these are among a priest's chief duties. Since "Christ is present when the Church prays and sings" (SC 7), the document begins by speaking about the Sunday assembly.

The preacher acts as a "mediator of meaning" who both represents the Lord and is attentive to the needs of the community. Well grounded in theological studies, knowledge of sacred Scripture, prayer, listening skills, and the social and economic culture, he preaches not so much *on* Scripture as *from* and *through* Scripture and gives "the community words of faith"(11). Since God's Word is living and active, speaking to us now, it summons a response from us—at the table of the Eucharist and in our daily lives.

To accomplish this, FYH stresses "non-negotiables" of homily preparation—prayer, biblical study, reflection, drafts, organization, revisions, concreteness, and frequent evaluation. It suggests the use of a homily preparation group (106–108).

Though one might be daunted by so great a task, the preacher is reminded that what he speaks is God's word and what he utters is God's wisdom (113). Finally, FYH calls for national and diocesan programs in homiletics and perhaps diocesan faculties to preach, so that there might be a renewal of preaching in the Church.

Introduction

The Assembly (1–15)

The Preacher (16–39)

The Homily (40–77)

Homiletic Method (78–111)

Epilogue: The Power of the Word (112–115)

Appendix (116–120)

GATHER FAITHFULLY TOGETHER

Roger Cardinal Mahoney, Archdiocese of Los Angeles

In anticipation of the Jubilee Year 2000, Roger Cardinal Mahoney of the Archdiocese of Los Angeles issued a pastoral letter on the Sunday Eucharist and how it is celebrated in the parish. "We have one central work to do: carry forward the renewal of Sunday Liturgy with vigor and joy. . . . This will not be one task among many. It will be *the* task of these next three years" (5, 6). Further, it would be the focus of all diocesan and parish leaders, working in collaboration.

He hailed the vision of Vatican II and the Constitution on the Sacred Liturgy. Calling it a "Pentecost for our time," he pledged to carry the work of renewal forward and to strengthen Sunday liturgy. "Lacking that effort, we have no center, no identity as the Body of Christ. With that effort, the renewal of every aspect of our Church life becomes possible" (12).

He recognized and named the tensions that exist between solemnity and community, external form and internal transformation, unity and diversity, and the challenges of many cultures present in his local church. In an excellent passage on inculturation (29–34) he asked his flock "to let the prevalent liturgy take on the pace, sounds, and shape that other cultures bring; and . . . to witness that in this Church there is finally no longer this people or that people, but one single assembly in Christ Jesus" (30).

Part 1 is a narrative of Sunday Mass at a theoretical parish, Our Lady of the Angels, in the summer of 2000. In rich imagery, he describes their gathering, their Liturgy of the Word, their Liturgy of the Eucharist, and their leave-taking. Within this narrative form, he sets standards of excellence "to kindle a passion for a vital Sunday Liturgy in every parish of our Archdiocese " (81). Further, he pledges support for training and personnel who will make that happen. He asks his pastors, especially, for better presiding, preaching, and leadership, including the hiring of a parish liturgy director.

Turning once again to the Constitution on the Sacred Liturgy (14), he elaborates on the full, conscious, and active participation which is the right and duty of all the baptized (GFT 88–100). This active participation means attention to each other and to the larger world (GFT 97–100). He describes liturgical ministry, beginning with the ministry of the assembly. Finally, he names five "steps" or "habits" that will engender life-giving liturgical practice Sunday after Sunday (GFT 105–110).

In Part Two, he sends a message to priests and others who have responsibility for the Sunday liturgy. First, he thanks them for the devotion already shown to the liturgy and exhorts them not to abandon the renewal but to move forward (116). This does not mean ignoring other pastoral issues. On

the contrary, by focusing on the liturgy "we will learn to do catechesis well
. . . this is how we will become people who see clearly where justice must
be done . . . and that building our liturgical practice is the only way we as
Catholics make our parish communities" (118). Most importantly, he asks
that they themselves become imbued with the spirit of the liturgy (123–127).

Cardinal Mahoney names the qualities of a model presider. First, the
presider *serves* the liturgy that his Church, in all its diversity, is celebrating.
He knows his assembly, is thoroughly prepared, is attentive to the liturgy,
and is engaged in the ritual. Second, the model presider respects symbol;
symbols are large and engaging and the symbolic deed is done with power
and reverence. Third, the presider has a liturgical piety, a spirit formed and
continually formed anew by the liturgy. The best catechesis he can provide
on the liturgy is the liturgy itself done well. The cardinal challenges his
presbyterate to improve the homily, the proclamation of the eucharistic
prayer, and celebration of the Communion Rite. The physical make-up of
the worship space, multilingual acclamations, and horizontal inclusive
language are three changes which, he contends, can and should be imple-
mented immediately.

Finally, he outlines a specific pastoral plan. By Pentecost of 1998 he expected parishes to conduct initial assessments and to name responsible personnel. By fall of 1998 each parish was to evaluate and improve five
areas—worship space, music, ministries, presiding, and preaching, and the
Mass schedule (178–183). By the First Sunday of Advent 1999 every Sunday
Liturgy was to be celebrated with the eucharistic prayer and the Communion Rite as described in this document.

He concludes, "The full and proper celebration of the Eucharist becomes
a powerful teacher for all of us, and the reverence, joy, participation, and silence of our celebrations deepen all of us in the life of Jesus Christ" (188).

Introduction (1–4)

> The Jubilee Year (5–7)
> The Vision of the Second Vatican Council (8–17)
> Start with Sunday Eucharist (18–23)
> Tensions (24–27)
> The Challenge and Blessing of Many Cultures (28–35)
> An Invitation (36–38)

Part One: A Message to All Catholics of the Archdiocese of Los Angeles

> Sunday Mass 2000 (39–79)
> From Here to There (80–110)

Part Two: A Message to Priests and Others Who Have Responsibility for the Sunday Liturgy

Conclusion

GOD'S MERCY ENDURES FOREVER: GUIDELINES ON THE PRESENTATION OF JEWS AND JUDAISM IN CATHOLIC PREACHING

Bishops' Committee on the Liturgy

Building on other documents which sought to promote understanding between Catholics and Jews, the Bishops' Committee on the Liturgy issued *God's Mercy Endures Forever*. The purpose of this brief document was to "assist the homilist . . . by indicating some of the major areas where challenges and opportunities occur and by offering perspectives and suggestions for dealing with them."

The first section pointed out the spiritual heritage shared by Christians and Jews and traced the Jewish roots of our Catholic liturgy. These include the liturgical year, prayer forms, vocabulary, Lectionary readings, etc.

The second section gives historical perspective to the biblical authors and the conflicts that existed in the first century between the primitive Church and Judaism. Two thousand years later, the Church calls for a renewed appreciation of the "dialogue between the first and second part of the Bible." Linking the saving acts of God among his chosen people with the saving acts of Jesus Christ, one can envision Jesus' ministry within the context of Second Temple Judaism.

Then the document "walks" the homilist through the liturgical year. In Advent, the readings link the eschatological hope of the Old Testament with the coming of the Messiah, Jesus Christ. Indeed, many Old Testament texts may be examined both from their historical context and from their christological applications. Next, the bishops offer new perspective to the Lenten readings, particularly the Gospel of Matthew and the treatment of the Pharisees. The Passion accounts of Holy Week should be read in comparison with one another since each brings new theological perspective (23). In the Easter season, particularly in the passages from Acts, the homilist will want to develop attitudes of reconciliation among his listeners.

The document includes suggestions for pastoral activities during Holy Week and the Easter season which may foster dialogue and understanding among Catholics and their Jewish neighbors. Finally, the bishops offer general principles for preaching throughout the year.

Introduction

Jewish Roots of the Liturgy (1–4)

Historical Perspectives and Contemporary Proclamation (5–10)

Advent: The Relationship between the Scriptures (11–15)

Lent: Controversies and Conflicts (16–20)

Holy Week: The Passion Narratives (21–25)

The Easter Season (26)

Pastoral Activity during Holy Week and the Easter Season (27–29)

Preaching Throughout the Year (30–32)

GUIDELINES FOR THE CELEBRATION OF THE SACRAMENTS WITH PERSONS WITH DISABILITIES

Catholics with disabilities often experienced inconsistencies in pastoral practices within and among dioceses. Were sign-language interpreters made available for the hearing-impaired community? Were church facilities accessible? Did catechetical programs exist for persons with developmental or mental disabilities? Drawing upon ritual texts, canonical tradition, and pastoral experience, the bishops of the United States formulated these guidelines to ensure greater consistency in the celebration of the sacraments with persons with disabilities and for fuller sacramental participation for all Catholics.

They begin by offering seven principles—(1) by reason of their baptism, all Catholics are equal in dignity; (2) Catholics with disabilities, who are otherwise properly disposed, may not be refused the sacraments; (3) parish sacramental celebrations should be accessible to all persons; (4) every effort should be made to determine the presence of persons with disabilities who reside within the parish boundaries; (5) parishes and dioceses should facilitate the evangelization, catechetical formation, and sacramental preparation for all persons with disabilities; (6) a parish should be fully accessible both in its attitude as well as its physical accommodations; and (7) dioceses should establish policies and procedures for making pastoral decisions in difficult cases.

The second section of the guideline delineates the special pastoral and physical needs of persons with disabilities as they approach each of the seven sacraments. This includes a comment that all persons in seminary formation be trained for service to the disabled community (33).

Preface

General Principles (1–7)

Particular Sacraments (8–39)

      Baptism (8–13)
      Confirmation (14–18)
      Eucharist (19–21)
      Reconciliation (22–25)
      Anointing of the Sick (26–29)
      Holy Orders (30–33)
      Marriage (34–39)

INCULTURATION AND THE ROMAN LITURGY: FOURTH INSTRUCTION FOR THE RIGHT APPLICATION OF THE CONCILIAR CONSTITUTION ON THE LITURGY, NOS. 37–40

Congregation for Divine Worship and Discipline of the Sacraments

In the years following the promulgation of the Constitution on the Sacred Liturgy, the CDW has issued instructions to clarify specific points in it. Issued in 1994, IRL is the fourth of those instructions. It is very limited in focus; it offers norms and principles for implementing articles 37–40, a section entitled "Norms for Adapting the Liturgy to the Culture and Traditions of Peoples."

Note the change in terminology from the 1963 original—"adapting" becomes "inculturation." The magisterium has defined inculturation as "the incarnation of the Gospel in autonomous cultures and at the same time the introduction of these cultures into the life of the Church." Adapting might mean simply "to modify," but *inculturation* implies a double movement—the Church introduces the Gospel into a culture and at the same time introduces the people and cultures into its own community (IRL 4). Inculturation has a dialogical character. "It is the fruit of progressive maturity in the faith of the people" (5).

Chapter I traces the role of inculturation throughout salvation history. Culture has always been a source of the expression of faith in the Old and New Testament. Jesus and his disciples proclaimed the Good News—to Jews and to Gentiles—within a particular context of history and culture. Christians continue to do the same. Liturgy, then, is not foreign to cultures, countries, or individuals, but "at the same time it should transcend the particularity of race or nation" (18).

Because, by its very nature, the liturgy is an action of Christ the High Priest and of his Church, it is grounded in the Word of God and in his sacraments. It is always the celebration of the paschal mystery of Jesus Christ, the glorification of God and the sanctification of mankind (21, 23, 24). Every particular Church is united to the universal Church by shared beliefs and uninterrupted apostolic tradition. The rule of prayer *(lex orandi)* corresponds to the rule of faith *(lex credendi)* (27).

Inculturation, then, presupposes the reception of Scripture into a given culture (28) and the careful pastoral analysis of its experience. Only then can a competent local authority introduce "into the liturgy such elements as are not bound up with superstition and error . . . provided they are in keeping with the true and authentic spirit of the liturgy" (IRL 31; cf. SC 37).

While the goal of inculturation is the full, conscious, and active participation of the faithful, at the same time, the Church's identity and mission must not be compromised. So chapter III provides principles, methods, and practical norms for the inculturation of the liturgy. Changes in texts and rites must preserve the inherent unity of the Roman Rite. Typical editions of liturgical books and translations approved by the Holy See are instruments of that unity.

There are various modes of adapting the liturgy—language, music, gestures, art, environment, etc., but IRL advises "necessary prudence." All innovations should "grow organically from forms already existing" (46). It cautions against syncretism—the juxtaposition of inappropriate non-Christian and Christian gestures or objects.

In chapter IV, IRL cites particular areas where adaptation is anticipated—the translation of texts from the typical edition (especially those texts which are sung), the gestures and postures of the faithful, regulations regarding the distribution of Communion, vestments, vessels, furnishings, the ordering of some rites, funeral rites, the liturgical year, and the Liturgy of the Hours (cf. GIRM Chapter IX).

The document concludes with procedures to follow for the approval of translations/adaptations. They include a process of experimentation supervised by an episcopal conference, the vote of the conference, and formal proposals to the Holy See.

Introduction (1–8)

I. Process of Inculturation throughout the History of Salvation (9–20)

II. Requirements of Preliminary Conditions for Inculturation (21–32)

    a) Requirements Emerging from the Nature of Liturgy
    b) Preliminary Conditions for Inculturation and the Liturgy
    c) The Responsibility of the Episcopal Conferences

III. Principles and Practical Norms for Inculturation of the Roman Rite (33–51)

    a) General Principles
    b) Adaptations Which Can Be Made
    c) Necessary Prudence

IV. Areas of Adaptation in the Roman Rite (52–69)

    a) Adaptations in the Liturgical Books
    b) Adaptations Envisaged by No. 40 at the Conciliar Constitution
        on the Liturgy

Conclusion

LITURGIAM AUTHENTICAM: FIFTH INSTRUCTION ON THE RIGHT APPLICATION OF THE CONCILIAR CONSTITUTION ON THE LITURGY

On December 4, 1963, the fathers of the Second Vatican Council approved the Constitution on the Sacred Liturgy. In the years following, the Holy See has published five documents, each named as an "Instruction for the Right Application of the Constitution on the Sacred Liturgy of the Second Vatican Council."

9-26-64   *Inter Oecumenici*—general principles for carrying out the liturgical renewal

5-4-97   *Tres abhinc annos*—adaptations to the Order of Mass

9-5-70   *Liturgicae instraurationes*—central role of the bishop in the renewal of the liturgy

1-25-94   *Varietates legitimae*—Roman liturgy and inculturation

3-28-01   *Liturgiam Authenticam*—regarding translation of the Roman liturgy

The last instruction further defines the provisions of article 36 of the constitution regarding vernacular translations. It seeks to preserve the identity and unity of the Roman Rite throughout the world. It suggests that the fourth and the fifth instruction be read in tandem. It discusses the choice of language for the vernacular text of a given region where a variety of languages exist; fidelity in rendering translations from the Latin *editiones typicae*; avoidance of modern modes of expression; the use of traditional collective terms; and the gender of the Persons of the Trinity.

Special consideration is given to the translation of scriptural texts. It clearly sets out the procedures for the approval of texts by conferences of bishops and for the review and confirmation by the CDW, noting especially the procedures for "mixed commissions," e.g., ICEL, a commission employed by conferences of English-speaking countries. It addresses the issues of new compositions, most notably hymns and chants. It concludes with a section on technicalities regarding copyright and publications.

Introduction: On the Use of Vernacular Languages in the Publication of the Books of the Roman Liturgy (1–9)

I. Choice of Vernacular Languages to Be Introduced into Liturgical Use (10–18)

II. On the Translation of Liturgical Texts into Vernacular Languages

General Principles Applied to All Translations (19–48)
Vocabulary (49–56)
Syntax, style and literary genre (57–62)
Norms applied to special types of texts
Eucharistic Prayers (63–64)
The Creed or Profession of Faith (65)
The *praenotanda* and the texts of a rubrical or juridic value (66–69)

III. On the Preparation of Translations and the Establishment of Commissions

The Manner of Preparing a Translation (70–78)
The Approbation of the Translation and the Petition for the *recognitio* of the Apostolic See (79–84)
On the Translation and Approbation of Sacramental Formulae (85–86)
On a Unified Version of the Liturgical Texts (87–91)
On Mixed Commissions (92–105)
The Composition of New Liturgical Texts in a Vernacular Language (106–108)

IV. The Publication of Liturgical Books (109–125)

V. The Translation of Proper Liturgical Texts

Diocesan Propers (126–127)
Propers of Religious Families (128–130)

Conclusion (131–133)

LITURGICAL MUSIC TODAY

Bishops' Committee on the Liturgy

Ten years after the promulgation of *Music in Catholic Worship* (1972), *Liturgical Music Today* addressed subjects not raised in the previous document and "a number of unforeseen issues in need of clarification and questions revealing new possibilities for liturgical music"(3). It should be read as a companion to MCW.

It begins with general principles—the structure of the liturgy; the place, function, and form of song; the pastoral concerns raised in MCW; and the unity of the Mass and its parts, especially the eucharistic prayer.

Then, LMT (with much greater depth than its predecessor) addresses music's role in the other sacraments and rites. In regard to the Liturgy of the Hours, it elaborates on GILH's musical comments and wisely counsels on the methods of singing psalms.

Finally, in "Other Matters" it discusses a wide range of issues—music and the rhythm of the Church year, music of the past, instrumental music, the use of recorded music, and copyright matters. In speaking of music ministers, LMT is the first to coin the phrase "pastoral musician."

Introduction (1–5)

General Principles (6–15)

Music in the Eucharist (16–21)

Music in the Celebration of Other Sacraments and Rites (22–33)

Music in the Liturgy of the Hours (34–45)

Other Matters (46–72)

Conclusion (73–74)

MUSIC IN CATHOLIC WORSHIP

Bishops' Committee on the Liturgy

More than forty years after its promulgation, liturgists and musicians rightfully treasure this document for its invaluable lessons.

It begins with a theology of celebration, noting how signs and symbols express faith. It counsels that pastoral planning is imperative for effective celebration. Both the liturgical celebration and the music that is integral to it, should be firmly rooted in Scripture, assess the needs and skills of the congregation and their presider, appreciate the occasion, and lead a diverse community to unity of purpose—the praise of the living God.

Chapter 3 is the most famous and enduring section of MCW. It reminds us that "music's function is ministerial; it must serve and never dominate" (23). The value of a musical selection is subject to a threefold judgment: the musical (nos. 26–29), liturgical (nos. 30–38), and pastoral (nos. 39–41). First, is the music artistically sound; is it suited to the liturgy? Second, does it serve the liturgy; does it express scriptural and liturgical texts correctly; how do various music ministers and instruments serve/enhance the liturgy? Third, is the music suitable to the time and occasion; is it sensitive to the ages, cultures, skills, and education of the assembly?

Part 4 offers general considerations on music and the various parts of the Mass, identifying those of primary and secondary importance. Part 5 elaborates on "more than a dozen parts" of the Mass that may be sung and distinguishes them by the nature and function of musical settings and selections.

The last section treats music used in communal sacramental celebrations, but is, regretfully, all too brief.

The Theology of Celebration (1–9)

Pastoral Planning for Celebration (10–22)

The Place of Music in the Celebration (23–41)

> Music Serves the Expression of Faith
> The Musical Judgment
> The Liturgical Judgment
> The Pastoral Judgment

General Considerations of Liturgical Structure (42–49)

Application of the Principles of Celebration to Music in Eucharistic Worship (50–78)

Music in Sacramental Celebrations (79–83)

PASCHALE SOLEMNITATIS: CIRCULAR LETTER ON PREPARING AND CELEBRATING THE PASCHAL FEASTS

Congregation for Divine Worship

A circular letter does not provide any new legislation, but rather collects and confirms what is already written. *Paschale Solemnitatis* is such a document. Gathering doctrinal, pastoral, and liturgical principles and blending them with commentary from the Roman Missal, the Constitution on the Sacred Liturgy, the *General Instruction of the Roman Missal, General Norms for the Liturgical Year and the Calendar,* and other documents and books, *Paschale Solemnitatis* educates the reader about Lent, the Triduum, and the Easter Season. "It is the aim of this document that the great mystery of our redemption be celebrated in the best possible way so that the faithful may participate in it with ever greater spiritual advantage" (5b).

Lent is a season with a double character—penitential and baptismal (SC 109). It prepares both the catechumens and the faithful to celebrate the paschal mystery. In general, PS stresses the importance of the Sundays of Lent (11) and encourages fine preaching on the season's rich Scriptures (11–12). It reminds planners to deemphasize flowers and music and to eliminate the *Alleluia.* Particular attention is paid to Ash Wednesday, the Sundays of Lent, and the optional use of Cycle A readings when celebrating the Scrutinies during Cycles B and C. Frequent penitential celebrations are encouraged throughout Lent.

Holy Week is actually not a "week" at all. It begins with Palm Sunday and ends on Thursday afternoon. Palm Sunday has a double "theme" of triumph and passion and the procession with palms should be executed only at the parish's most populous Mass. Central to this liturgy is the proclamation of the Passion account. Finally, the diocesan Chrism Mass is preferably celebrated on Holy Thursday; holy oils, blessed and consecrated at the Mass of Chrism, are brought back to the parish and presented before the Evening Mass of the Lord's Supper.

Chapter IV (38–43) gives an overview of the Easter Triduum—one liturgy celebrated over three days. PS notes the importance of preparation, sufficient ministers, singing, and encourages fasting and abstinence.

The Holy Thursday Evening Mass of the Lord's Supper is treated in chapter V (44–57). Drawing from the text in the Sacramentary, PS notes that on this night we commemorate the institution of the Eucharist, the institution of the priesthood, and loving service to one another. (Actually, in the pericope from John's Gospel, the *mandatum* is emphasized—Jesus' command to love one another. Perhaps here, the "self-giving" nature of the Eucharist and the ministerial priesthood is also evident.) PS gives clear directives for the proper time of the celebration, the tabernacle, the place of reservation, the *Gloria*, musical instruments, the washing of the feet, gifts for the poor, Communion to the homebound, procession to the place of reservation, the stripping of the altar, and the extinguishing of lamps.

On Good Friday (58–72), the Church "meditates on the Passion of Christ." All sacramental celebrations are prohibited this day except for the anointing of the sick and for penance (66, 75). The liturgy continues at "around three o'clock." PS gives norms for the three-part celebration—the Liturgy of the Word, the Veneration of the Cross, and Holy Communion. Chapter VII (73–76) briefly treats Holy Saturday as a day of meditation.

Chapter VIII addresses Easter, emphasizing the nocturnal nature of its Vigil (77–80) in which we "wait for the coming of the Lord" (80). Read, with great care, articles 81–92. They describe the Easter Vigil and the significance of its parts—the Service of the Light, the Liturgy of the Word, the Liturgy of Initiation, and the Liturgy of the Eucharist. Pastoral considerations are abundant, especially the directive that smaller parishes gather together to celebrate the Vigil. Easter Day (97–98) is to be celebrated with great solemnity and should include the Sprinkling Rite, the renewal of baptismal promises, and a communal celebration of Easter Vespers. The paschal candle maintains a special place of honor until Pentecost (99).

In chapter IX (100–108), PS reminds us that the Easter celebration continues for fifty days and is a special time for our neophytes. Solemn First Communion, the blessing of homes, and Communion to the sick take on special significance in parish life in this joyful season.

Most of all, PS stresses that the Triduum and the seasons which surround it, are best characterized by communal celebrations that manifest the very nature of the Church. The careful reading of this document is imperative for those who prepare, preside over, and participate in the Great Ninety Days.

Preface (1–5)

I. Lenten Season (6–26)

> Concerning the Rites of Initiation
> Celebrations during the Lenten Season
> Particular Details Concerning the Days of Lent

II. Holy Week (27–37)

> Passion Sunday (Palm Sunday)
> The Chrism Mass
> The Penitential Celebrations in Lent

III. The Easter Triduum in General (38–43)

IV. Holy Thursday Evening Mass of the Lord's Supper (44–57)

V. Good Friday (58–72)

VI. Holy Saturday (73–76)

VII. Easter Sunday of the Lord's Resurrection (77–99)

> The Easter Vigil
> > a) The Meaning of the Nocturnal Character of the Easter Vigil
> > b) The Structure of the Easter Vigil and the Significance of Its
> > Different Elements and Parts
> > c) Some Pastoral Considerations
> Easter Day

VIII. Easter Time (100–108)

PLENTY GOOD ROOM: THE SPIRIT AND TRUTH
OF AFRICAN AMERICAN CATHOLIC WORSHIP

Secretariat for Liturgy and the Secretariat for Black Catholics

The first two sections of *Plenty Good Room* offer a brilliant overview of liturgy, analyzing ritual, signs, and symbols, and the centrality of the paschal mystery.

Since the goal of liturgical adaptation has always been to "intensify the experience of the mystery of Christ and God's saving power for all peoples" (13), the authors then present a history lesson on cultural adaptation from the early Church to Vatican II. They conclude that the Church does not wish to impart "a rigid uniformity in liturgical expression," but rather welcomes adaptations "provided they are in keeping with the true and authentic spirit of the liturgy" (PGR #24; SC 37). These legitimate variations, accompanied by catechesis, play a vital role in evangelization.

Since cultural pluralism is not only legitimate but desirable, PGR quotes both Pope Paul VI and Pope John Paul II in their call for African expression to further the "Catholic nature that is the Church's" (PGR #31). European culture, due to strong missionary activity in recent centuries, may have become the normative culture of the Church, but all people have a culture (39).

Focusing on the African American Church, PGR notes that although African Americans are "a varied people," they share a heritage of slavery and racism and the "invisible institution" that sustained them. Firmly rooted in Scripture and forged in storytelling, theirs is a unique spirituality.

Authentic African American Catholic worship is centered on Word and sacrament. It has its own spirituality, born of conversion, that is characterized as contemplative, holistic, joyful, and communitarian. It relishes emotion as a way of learning. This culture's ritual activity, then, expresses a unique vision of space, time, action, language, preaching, and sacred song.

Recognizing the importance of the Sunday assembly and rooted in sound principles of cultural adaptation, PGR proposes the pastoral *In Spirit and Truth* as a signpost and model of worship. It concludes by offering, from it, rituals and texts that might serve as effective models for adaptation to the Roman Liturgy.

I. Liturgy and Symbolic Reality (1–10)

II. Liturgy and the Christ Event (11–13)

III. Liturgy and Culture (14–28)

IV. Liturgical Adaptation in the African American Community (29–42)

V. The African American Religious Experience in the United States (43–68)

VI. The African American Church (69–76)

VII. Toward an Authentic African American Catholic Worship (77–104)

VIII. An African American Catholic Worship Model: *In Spirit and Truth* (105–124)

TO SPEAK AS A CHRISTIAN COMMUNITY: PASTORAL MESSAGE ON INCLUSIVE LANGUAGE

The Pastoral Team of the Canadian Conference of Catholic Bishops

In this brief, but profound document, inclusive language was broadly defined to mean "using words which affirm the equality and dignity of each person regardless of race, gender, creed, age, or ability" (2). As a guide to those who were charged with translating liturgical texts, it focused primarily on nonsexist language and the fundamental equality of men and women. Ever conscious of social context, it asked Christians to read the "signs of the times."

Since the Church by its very nature is a communion—we in union with God and with one another, through Christ and in the Holy Spirit—we must be a sign or sacrament of that unity (6). The bishops encouraged those who translate biblical and liturgical texts to employ experts in theology, history, linguistics, and even archeology to uncover the depths of original texts and to apply their meaning to our modern age. Approving liturgical texts may require a lengthy process, but the use of inclusive language in homes, at gatherings, in hymns, intercessions, and homilies may and should be immediate.

This document called for fidelity to tradition and spoke against discrimination—truly the pastoral message was aptly named.

Introduction (1)

Inclusive Language Defined (2)

Sign of the Times (3)

Language Expresses Our Beliefs (4)

Fundamental Equality of Men and Women (5)

The Church as Communion (6)

Implementation—Long Term (7)

Biblical and Liturgical Texts (8)

Evolution of Language (9)

Levels of Awareness (10)

Implementation—Short Term (11)

Conclusion (12)

FOR FURTHER READING: CHAPTERS IV AND V

Adam, Adolf. *The Liturgical Year: Its History and Its Meaning After the Reform of the Liturgy.* Trans. Matthew J. O'Connell. Collegeville: The Liturgical Press/Pueblo Publishing Company, 1981, 1990.

Bonneau, Normand. *The Sunday Lectionary: Ritual Word, Paschal Shape.* Collegeville: The Liturgical Press, 1998.

Boyer, Mark. *The Liturgical Environment: What the Documents Say.* Collegeville: The Liturgical Press, 1990.

Chupungo, Anscar. *Liturgical Inculturation: Sacramentals, Religiosity, and Catechesis.* Collegeville: The Liturgical Press/Pueblo Publishing Company, 1992.

Deiss, Lucien. *Visions of Liturgy and Music for a New Century.* Collegeville: The Liturgical Press, 1996.

Foley, Edward. *Ritual Music: Studies in Liturgical Musicology.* Beltsville, Md.: The Pastoral Press, 1995.

Foley, Edward, and Mary McGann. *Music and the Eucharistic Prayer.* American Essays in Liturgy. Collegeville: The Liturgical Press, 1988.

Francis, Mark. *A Guide to Inculturation and the Liturgy.* Washington, D.C.: Federation of Diocesan Liturgical Commissions, 1997.

Fuller, Reginald. *Preaching the Lectionary: The Word of God for the Church Today.* Collegeville: The Liturgical Press, 1984.

Giles, Richard. *Re-pitching the Tent: Reordering the Church Building for Worship and Mission.* Collegeville: The Liturgical Press, 1999.

Hoffman, Elizabeth, ed. *The Liturgy Documents: A Parish Resource, Volume One.* Archdiocese of Chicago: Liturgy Training Publications, 1991.

Huels, John. *Disputed Questions in the Liturgy Today.* Archdiocese of Chicago: Liturgy Training Publications, 1988.

———. *More Disputed Questions in the Liturgy Today.* Archdiocese of Chicago: Liturgy Training Publications, 1990.

Joncas, Jan Michael. *From Sacred Song to Ritual Music: Twentieth-Century Understandings of Roman Catholic Worship Music.* Collegeville: The Liturgical Press, 1997.

Leaver, Robin, and Joyce Ann Zimmerman, eds. *Liturgy and Music.* Lifetime Learning. Collegeville: The Liturgical Press, 1998.

Leonard, John, and Nathan Mitchell. *The Postures of the Assembly During the Eucharistic Prayer.* A Project of the Notre Dame Center for Pastoral Liturgy. Archdiocese of Chicago: Liturgy Training Publications, 1994.

Lysik, David, ed. *The Liturgy Documents: A Parish Resource, Volume Two.* Archdiocese of Chicago: Liturgy Training Publications, 1999.

Mick, Lawrence. *Worshiping Well: A Mass Guide for Planners and Participants.* Collegeville: The Liturgical Press, 1998.

Secretariat, Bishops' Committee on the Liturgy. *Ceremonial of Bishops, A Reader: Proceedings of the National Workshop on the Ceremonial of Bishops*. Washington, D.C.: United States Catholic Conference, Inc., 1994.

Smolarski, Dennis. *The General Instruction of the Roman Missal: A Commentary*. Collegeville: The Liturgical Press, 2003.

Talley, Thomas J. *The Origins of the Liturgical Year*. New York: Pueblo Publishing Company, 1986.

Waznak, Robert. *An Introduction to the Homily*. Collegeville: The Liturgical Press, 1998.

Audiovisual

"Gather Faithfully Together," a video based on the pastoral letter by Roger Cardinal Mahoney, Archdiocese of Los Angeles, 1997.

Chapter VI

Decisions, Decisions, Decisions

The previous chapters have acquainted the reader with the Church's liturgical books and some of her liturgical documents. This chapter will offer general principles that will assist you in what must now appear to be an overwhelming task—to decide among the wealth of prayer texts, readings, and information available. The following chapters, then, will offer specific citations and suggestions for individual liturgies.

As you begin to prepare a parish liturgy, the first question you must always ask is "What is the rest of the Church celebrating today?"

LITURGICAL YEAR

We measure our lifetimes with the passing of months, years, decades, birthdays, silver anniversaries, or golden jubilees. We think in terms of duration; we might call this time *chronos* (from this word we get chronological). But we can also measure time in relation to personal actions or events, such as the birth of our children, "when we were newlyweds," or "when we lived in Boston." This brings us a little closer to the concept of *kairos* time, how the Church measures time—a time filled with meaning by God.

The "event" that gives all time meaning is the salvific action of Jesus Christ; all other events in salvation history lead from it and to it. Our liturgical celebrations, then, are not mere recollections or dramatizations of this past event; they are anamnesis in the strongest sense of this word—a remembering that makes this event *present* to us here and now. The paschal mystery of Christ's passion, death, and resurrection gives meaning to our celebrations; we "wait in joyful hope" for the eschaton when "God will be all in all." The paschal mystery is so immense that we take a year to explore all its facets. It permeates seasons, weeks, days, even hours. We call this our liturgical year.

> Christ's saving work is celebrated in sacred memory by the Church on fixed days throughout the year. Each week on the day called the Lord's Day the Church commemorates the Lord's resurrection. Once a year at Easter the Church honors this resurrection and passion with the utmost solemnity. In fact, through the yearly cycle the Church unfolds the entire mystery of Christ and keeps the anniversary of the saints . . . (GNLYC 1).

The document entitled *General Norms for the Liturgical Year and the Calendar* elaborates on the structure of the Church year (3–16) beginning with a treatise on the importance of Sunday (4–7). Special days of the year are ranked according to their importance—solemnities, feasts, obligatory memorials, and optional memorials. Solemnities are very special days on the calendar that focus on an important event in the life of Christ, on one of

Christ's titles, or on a prominent saint. These days have a vigil, that is, their observance begins the evening before. The two great solemnities, Easter and Christmas, also have their own octave, i.e., the solemnity continues for eight days. Finally, there are days we simply refer to as "weekdays"—days that follow Sunday (GNLYC 16). They, too, are ranked according to the season in which they occur.

The Church collects these days into a yearly cycle of seasons. The Proper of Seasons includes Advent, the Christmas season, Lent, Triduum, the Easter season, and Ordinary Time. Ordinary Time is not plain or unimportant. It is so named because it is "counted" time; *ordo* means "to put in order."

All of this is included in the Church's *General Calendar*, so called because it is observed by the universal Church. There are two perspectives to this calendar—the temporal cycle and the sanctoral cycle. In the former the Church celebrates the mystery of Christ. In the latter, it celebrates the saints in whom we have communion with Christ. These two "cycles" are concurrent—independent of one another, but not necessarily mutually exclusive—since all our liturgies celebrate the paschal mystery.

The Church also permits the addition of a *particular calendar*—one in which the local diocese or a religious congregation may designate special days to honor a saint or celebrate an event of interest to them (GNLYC 48–55).

During the different seasons, the Church may "carry out the formation of the faithful by means of devotional practices . . . instruction, and works of penance and mercy" (GNLYC 2). It does so in harmony with the year's liturgical celebrations (SC 13). For example, in the USA, the bishops have named January 22 as a day of penance for acts against the dignity of life caused by abortion.

With such a rich variety of celebrations in twelve short months, how do you keep it all straight? The following table may help you understand the days of the liturgical year and their order of importance.

TABLE OF LITURGICAL DAYS
ACCORDING TO THEIR ORDER OF PRECEDENCE

GENERAL NORMS FOR THE LITURGICAL YEAR AND THE CALENDAR #59

I.

1. Easter Triduum of the Lord's Passion and Resurrection

2. Christmas, Epiphany, Ascension, and Pentecost
   Sundays of Advent, Lent, and the Easter season
   Ash Wednesday
   Weekdays of Holy Week from Monday to Thursday inclusive
   Days within the Octave of Easter

3. Solemnities of the Lord, The Blessed Virgin Mary, and saints listed in the General Calendar
   All Souls (Commemoration of All the Faithful Departed)

4. Proper Solemnities, namely:
   a. Solemnity of the principal patron of the place, i.e., the city or state
   b. Solemnity of the dedication of a particular church and the anniversary
   c. Solemnity of the title of a particular church
   d. Solemnity of the title, or of the founder, or of the principal patron of a religious order

II.

5. Feasts of the Lord in the General Calendar

6. Sundays of the Christmas season and Sundays in Ordinary Time

7. Feasts of the Blessed Virgin Mary and of the saints in the General Calendar

8. Proper Feasts, namely:
   a. Feast of the principal patron of the diocese
   b. Feast of the anniversary of the dedication of the cathedral
   c. Feast of the principal patron of a region or province, or a country, or of a wider territory
   d. Feast of the title, founder, or principal patron of an order or congregation and of a religious province, without prejudice to the directives in no. 4.
   e. Other feasts proper to an individual church
   f. Other feasts listed in the calendar of a diocese or of a religious order or congregation

9. Weekdays of Advent from 17 December to 24 December, inclusive.
Days within the Octave of Christmas.
Weekdays of Lent

III.

10. Obligatory memorials in the General Calendar

11. Proper obligatory memorials, namely:
    a. Memorial of a secondary patron of the place, diocese, region,
       or province, country or wider territory, or of an order or
       congregation and of a religious province
    b. Obligatory memorials listed in the calendar of a diocese,
       or of an order or congregation

12. Optional Memorials; but these may be celebrated even on the days
listed in no. 9, in the special manner described by the *General Instruction of
the Roman Missal* and of the Liturgy of the Hours.
    In the same manner obligatory memorials may be celebrated as op-
tional memorials if they happen to fall on the Lenten weekdays.

13. Weekdays of Advent up to 16 December inclusive
    Weekdays of the Christmas season from 2 January until the Saturday
       after Epiphany
    Weekdays of the Easter season from Monday after the octave of
       Easter until the Saturday before Pentecost inclusive
    Weekdays in Ordinary Time

If several celebrations fall on the same day, the one that holds the highest
rank according to the above table is observed. "But a solemnity impeded by
a liturgical day that takes precedence over it should be transferred to the clos-
est day not listed in nos. 1–8 in the table of the precedence; the rule of no. 5 remains in effect. Other celebrations are omitted that year" (GNLYC 60).
    If you are preparing a celebration of the Liturgy of the Hours, you may
find a reference to "EP I" and "EP II." A Sunday or solemnity may have an
Evening Prayer for the evening before as well as for the day itself. If two
special days coincide, and a day calls both for Evening Prayer of that day's
office and Evening Prayer I of the following day, Evening Prayer of the day
with the higher rank takes precedence. In cases of equal rank, Evening
Prayer of the actual day takes precedence (GNLYC 61; see also SC 13; LMT
48; DD 3, 21–22, 64, 75, 80; PS 3–4).

THE CHOICE OF THE MASS AND ITS PARTS

The pastoral effectiveness of a celebration will be greatly increased if the texts of the readings, the prayers, and the liturgical songs correspond as closely as possible to the needs, spiritual preparation, and culture of those taking part. . . .

The priest, therefore, in planning the celebration of Mass, should have in mind the common spiritual good of the people of God, rather than his own inclinations. He should, moreover, remember that the selection of different parts is to be made in agreement with those who have some role in the celebration, including the faithful, in regard to the parts that more directly pertain to each.

Since, indeed, a variety of options is provided for the different parts of the Mass, it is necessary for the deacon, the lectors, the psalmist, the cantor, the commentator, and choir to be completely sure before the celebration about those texts for which each is responsible is to be used and that nothing be improvised. Harmonious planning and carrying out of the rites will be of great assistance in disposing the faithful to take part in the Eucharist (GIRM 352).

In General: Choice of Mass

After choosing the liturgical day, you will want to be familiar with the regulations in the *General Instruction of the Roman Missal,* particularly those found in chapter 7, "The Choice of the Mass and Its Parts."

It notes that on solemnities a priest is bound to follow the calendar of the Church where he is celebrating (GIRM 353). On Sundays, on feasts, obligatory memorials, and the weekdays of the seasons of Advent, Christmas, Lent, and Easter, he is obliged to follow the calendar when celebrating Mass with a congregation (GIRM 354). Various options and restrictions are given on days which are listed as optional memorials (GIRM 355).

Pastors are bound to celebrate Mass on Sundays and holy days for the faithful entrusted to their care.

In general, the priest and those who assist him in planning liturgies should not omit too frequently the assigned readings from the Lectionary so "that a richer portion of the table of God's word might be provided for the people" (GIRM 355).

Masses and Prayers for Various Circumstances

Since the liturgy of the Sacraments and Sacramentals causes, for the faithful who are properly disposed, almost every event in life to be sanctified by divine grace that flows from the paschal mystery, and because the Eucharist is the Sacrament of Sacraments, the Missal provides formularies for Masses and orations that may be used in various circumstances of Christian life, for the needs of the world, or for the needs of the Church . . . (GIRM 368).

Masses for Various Circumstances: Ritual Masses, Masses for Various Needs, Masses for Various Circumstances, and Votive Masses (GIRM 371)

Ritual Masses are connected with certain sacraments or sacramentals. They are prohibited on Sundays of Advent, Lent, and Easter, on solemnities, on days within the octave of Easter, on All Souls', on Ash Wednesday, and during Holy Week (GIRM 372).

Masses for Various Needs or Masses for Various Circumstances can be used as special occasions arise or at fixed times (GIRM 373). Special days of prayer may be established by the conference of bishops and may use these Mass texts (e.g., January 22 in the USA). Masses for Various Needs and Circumstances may not be celebrated on solemnities; Sundays of Advent, Lent, and Easter; days within the octave of Easter, All Souls', Ash Wednesday, and Holy Week (GIRM 374).

Votive Masses, related to a mystery of the Lord or in honor of the Blessed Virgin Mary, the angels or the saints, may be said for the sake of the faithful's devotion (GIRM 375) on weekdays in Ordinary Time, even on optional memorials. On Saturdays of Ordinary Time, which are designated simply as "weekdays," a Mass in honor of the BVM may be offered (GIRM 378).

Unless there is some grave need, the use of Masses for Various Needs, Masses for Various Circumstances, and Votive Masses are forbidden on obligatory memorials, weekdays of Advent up to December 16, weekdays in the Christmas season after January 2, and in the Easter season after the Octave.

Masses for the Dead

Masses for the Dead are to be used "in moderation, since every Mass is offered for both the living and the dead, and there is a commemoration of the dead in the Eucharistic Prayer" (GIRM 355).

The funeral Mass holds first place among the Masses for the Dead and may be celebrated any day "except on solemnities that are days of obligation, Holy Thursday, the Easter Triduum, and the Sundays of Advent, Lent, and Easter"(GIRM 380). When they are permitted, Masses for the Dead may also be offered upon "receiving the news of a death, for the final burial, or on the first anniversary, even on days within the octave of Christmas, on obligatory memorials, and on weekdays, except for Ash Wednesday or weekdays during Holy Week" (GIRM 381).

The chart on the following page summarizes the above.

TABLE OF RUBRICS GOVERNING THE USE OF RITUAL MASSES, MASSES FOR VARIOUS NEEDS, MASSES FOR VARIOUS CIRCUMSTANCES, AND MASSES FOR THE DEAD

V1 = Ritual Masses (GIRM 372); MVNO and VM in case of serious pastoral need or advantage at the direction of the local ordinary or with his permission (GIRM 374 and 376)

V2 = MVNO and VM in cases of serious need or pastoral advantage, at the discretion of the rector of the church or the priest celebrant (GIRM 376 and 376)

V3 = MVNO and VM chosen by the priest celebrant in favor of the devotion of the people (GIRM 377)

R1 = Funeral Mass (GIRM 380)

R2 = Mass on the occasion of news of a death, final burial, or the first anniversary (GIRM 381)

R3 = Daily Mass for the Dead (GIRM 355, 379, 381). When R1 and R2 are not permitted, neither is R3.

(+) = permitted   (-) = not permitted

Solemnities of precept	V1 -	R1 -
Sundays of Advent, Lent, and the Easter Season	V1 -	R1 -
Holy Thursday, Easter Triduum	V1 -	R1 -
Solemnities not of precept, All Souls	V1 -	R1 +
Ash Wednesday, weekdays of Holy Week	V1 -	R1 +
Days in the Easter Octave	V1 -	R1 +
Sundays of Christmas, and in Ordinary Time	V1+, V2-	R1+, R2-
Feasts	V1+, V2-	R1+, R2-
Weekdays December 17–24	V1+, V2-	R1+, R2+
Days in the Christmas Octave	V1+, V2-	R1+, R2+
Weekdays of Lent	V1+, V2-	R1+, R2+
Obligatory Memorials	V1+, V2+	R1+, R2+
Weekdays of Advent to December 16	V1+, V2+	R1+, R2+
Weekdays of Christmas from January 2	V1+, V2+	R1+, R2+
Weekdays of the Easter Season	V1+, V2+	R1+, R2+
Weekdays in Ordinary Time	V1+, V2+, V3+	R1+, R2+, R3+

Adapted from Appendix III, *Ceremonial of Bishops* © ICEL

The Choice of Readings

The *Lectionary for Mass* has assigned three readings to Sundays and Solemnities—one from a prophet, an apostle, and a Gospel (GIRM 357). These readings (or the options allowed) must be strictly followed.

On feasts and memorials, two readings are assigned; a third reading may be added if the day is raised to the rank of a solemnity (e.g., as a parish patronal feast). Unless feasts or memorials have their own proper readings, the readings from a Commons or the readings of the day may be used (GIRM 357).

In volumes II and III of the *Lectionary for Mass,* readings are provided for every weekday of the year. On occasion, the continuous reading for weekdays is interrupted by the observance of a solemnity, feast, or memorial. In this case the priest may combine omitted parts with other readings or decide which readings are to be preferred (GIRM 358).

Ritual Masses, Masses for Various Needs, Masses for Various Circumstances, Votive Masses, and Masses for the Dead have their own suggested readings (GIRM 359). Consult each pertinent section of the *Lectionary for Mass, Volume IV.*

When long and short forms are given for a particular reading, pastors and their planning teams may wish to consider both the capacity of the assembly and the requirements of the homily (GIRM 360, 361).

The Choice of Orations

Some parts of the Mass are variable. The prayers unique to each Mass are the Opening Prayer (or Collect), the Prayer Over The Gifts, and the Prayer After Communion.

On the memorial of saints, the Opening Prayer can be found in the Sacramentary either in the Propers of the Saints or the Commons. The Prayer Over the Gifts and the Prayer After Communion may also be located in the Proper, the Commons or, if it is lacking, from a weekday in that season (GIRM 363).

On the weekdays in Ordinary Time, the prayers can be taken from the preceding Sunday, from any Sunday, or from Masses for Various Needs (ibid.).

The Prayer of the Faithful (The Universal Prayer or the General Intercessions) should be composed for each liturgy with a congregation. Samples are printed in Appendix I of the Sacramentary. In general, they should be offered first for the Church, then for public authorities and the salvation of the world, for those oppressed by various needs, for the dead, and for the local community (GIRM 69).

Choice of the Eucharistic Prayer

The Church has ten official eucharistic prayers. Some of the eucharistic prayers have their own preface. Some have the option of substituting a proper preface. The prefaces may be found in the Sacramentary and, by being more specific to the commemoration or to the season of the liturgical year, a specific preface may "bring out more fully the motives for thanksgiving within the Eucharistic Prayer and to set out more clearly the different facets of the mystery of salvation" (GIRM 364).

The choice of the Eucharistic Prayer may be guided by the following (GIRM 365):

Eucharistic Prayer I (The Roman Canon)	may be used any day on a day when there are special embolisms on celebrations of the Apostles or Saints on any Sunday
Eucharistic Prayer II	is suited for weekdays, special circumstances has its own Preface but may use others may add an embolism in Masses for the Dead
Eucharistic Prayer III	may be said with any Preface suited to Sundays or major feasts may add special formula for the Dead
Eucharistic Prayer IV	has an unchangeable preface gives a full summary of salvation history may be used on Sundays in Ordinary Time may be used when a Mass has no proper preface
Eucharistic Prayer MVNO	may be used at any of the Masses for a Various Need or Circumstance has its own proper preface(s) These four prefaces and their matching set of intercessions can create variety within this one prayer.

Eucharistic Prayers for Masses with Children (C1, C2, C3) and Eucharistic Prayers for Masses of Reconciliation (R1 and R2) have their own proper preface so they cannot be used on days when a proper preface is given in the Roman Missal.

How to Use an Ordo

July 20 Saturday: Weekday [15]; *BVM on Saturday*
m   HOURS   Pss III   Seasonal wkdy   *Common of BVM*
Gr   *on Sat*   EP 1 of Sun: begin Pss IV
Wh   MASS   any Mass *or of mem*   Sugg: *Holy Mary, Handmaid*
V3 R3   *of the Lord (Collection, #22); 9 alt*
         RDGS   394: Mi 2:1-5   Ps 10:1-4, 7-8, 14   Mt 12:14-21
Social injustice (Ps) is denounced by Micah (1). The suffering servant seeks
faith, not superficial enthusiasm (2).

March 19 Tuesday: JOSEPH, HUSBAND OF THE VIRGIN MARY
S   HOURS*   Sanctoral Prop   Common of Holy Men
Wh   MP: Proper antt   Pss Sun I   DP: proper antt
R1   compl Pss   NP: Sun II
         MASS   Prop   Gl   Cr   Pf of Joseph
         RDGS   543: 2 Sm 7:4-5a, 12-14a, 16   Ps 89:2-5, 27,29
                    Rom 4: 13, 16-18, 22   Mt 1:16, 18-21, 24a or
                    Luke 2:41-51a

An heir of David (1, Ps) and son of Joseph and Mary (3b), Jesus brings forgiveness (3a) through the gift of faith (2).

Joseph honored on 19 March since the end of the 10th c; declared Patron of the Universal Church in 1870 by Pope Pius IX; patron of workers and carpenters; also of Austria, Belgium, Bohemia, Canada, Mexico, Peru and (South) Vietnam; mentioned in the Roman Canon.

PN It is the custom in some places today to bless bread, pastries, and other food and to give a large portion to the poor. For the Order of Blessing of St. Joseph's Table, see BB nos. 1679–1700.

Source: *The Order of Prayer in the Liturgy of the Hours and Celebration of the Eucharist 2002.* Compiled by Peter Rocca, C.S.C. Mahwah, N.J.: Paulist Press, 2001, 73, 161.

The boxes above are entries from an *ordo*. From the Latin for "arrangement," this little book can be an invaluable tool for those who prepare liturgy. It provides a wealth of information in a very compact format.

Ordos can be purchased from a variety of publishers or religious houses. They can vary in format and in the amount of information they provide. Often, ordos are produced for various dioceses or regions so that they might reflect that area's particular liturgical calendar. Each ordo may use its own set of symbols or abbreviations, so consult the key provided in the front (or back) of the book.

Examine the samples above. In the first box, one reads that on Saturday, July 20, a weekday in the Fifteenth Week in Ordinary Time, any Mass may be used. Indeed, on any Saturday in Ordinary Time that does not have a prescribed feast or memorial, a Mass of the BVM is optional (cf. GIRM 375). V3 allows Masses for Various Needs and Occasions or a Votive Mass. R3 means that a Mass for the Dead may be offered. The *ordo* tells you that this is Week III of the four-week Psalter and on Saturday night you will use Evening Prayer I for Sunday of Week IV. The readings for the day are found in the Lectionary #394; a brief summary of each is provided. The Mass vestments may be green or white, depending on your choice of Mass.

On the other hand, the *ordo* provides strict guidelines for March 19, the Solemnity of Joseph, Husband of Mary. There are proper prayers for this solemnity, including a proper preface (Preface #62). Even though this solemnity falls in Lent, the *Gloria* is sung. The Creed is professed. There is additional information about St. Joseph and pastoral notes mention a special blessing for food which is distributed to the poor.

What other information can you find in these samples?

Choice of Music

> The musical tradition of the universal Church is a treasure of inestimable value, greater even than that of any other art. The main reason for this preeminence is that, as sacred song closely bound to the text, it forms a necessary or integral part of the solemn liturgy.
>
> Holy Scripture itself has bestowed praise upon sacred song and the same may be said of the Fathers of the Church and of the Roman Pontiffs who in recent years, led by St. Pius X, have explained more precisely the ministerial function supplied by sacred music in the service of the Lord.
>
> Therefore sacred music will be the more holy the more closely it is joined to the liturgical rite, whether by adding delight to prayer, fostering oneness of spirit, or investing the rites with greater solemnity . . . (SC 112).

Music is integral to the liturgy and, therefore, the choice of music is integral to any discussion on the preparation of liturgical prayer. This small space could not thoroughly educate the reader about the role of music in the liturgy, offer suggestions for repertoire, or give a historical survey on the Church's rich treasury of sacred music. But since it is a book about resources on the liturgy, it will offer a glimpse into basic principles and suggest what one might read to better prepare the Church's liturgy.

"What parts do we sing?"

The four-hymn pattern developed in the context of the Latin Mass. That was one of the few ways the people could participate in the vernacular. But since the constitution called for more ways to foster the full, conscious, and active participation of the faithful, the new Order of Mass has more than a dozen parts which may be sung as well as numerous options for the celebrant. Each has its own nature and function (MCW 52).

Acclamations are "shouts of joy" from the assembly and by their nature they should be strong, melodically appealing, and affirmative (MCW 53). The people should know these by heart and be able to master a wide variety of them. There are five of them in the Mass (MCW 55–59):

1) The *Alleluia* before (and after) the gospel. If this is not sung it should be omitted. In Lent, a brief acclamatory verse replaces it.
2) The *Holy, holy, holy* is the people's acclamation of praise which concludes the preface.
3) The *memorial acclamation* expresses our faith in the paschal mystery.
4) With the *Great Amen* we assent to the Eucharistic prayer and make it our own.
5) The doxology to the Lord's Prayer is a prayer of praise added to the words of Jesus.

(For more on acclamations, cf. SC 30; GIRM 34–37, 79, 128, 147, 216; MCW 47, 53–59; LMT 15–17, 90–91; DMC 30–31.)

Processional songs, i.e., the Entrance Song and the Communion Song, produce a sense of community. The Entrance Song should create a sense of celebration and help the people prepare to hear the word of God (MCW 61). The Communion Song(s) should foster a sense of unity. While it may be seasonal in nature during Advent, Lent, the Christmas season, and the Easter season, the Communion Song should primarily remind us of our unity in the Body of Christ, the fruit of Holy Communion (MCW 62).

The **responsorial psalm** or "chant between the readings" fosters meditation on the Word of God (GIRM 61). It should be proclaimed at the ambo. The text should, as a rule, be taken from the Lectionary. One may not substitute a hymn based on a psalm (ibid.). A single, pertinent psalm may be used throughout one of the major seasons of the Church year.

Ordinary chants. The *Lord have mercy* or *Kyrie* (Greek) is a traditional prayer of praise to the risen Lord that invokes his mercy. It may be used in a six-fold style, a nine-fold pattern or incorporated into the penitential rite. The *Glory to God* is usually restricted to Sundays outside of Lent and Advent and on solemnities and feasts. It may be recited, but it should be sung (GIRM 53). The Lord's Prayer is an immediate preparation for Communion

(GIRM 81). The *Lamb of God* is a litany to accompany the Breaking of the Bread (GIRM 81). Tropes may be added as necessary to cover the ritual action. The *Profession of Faith* or Creed may also be sung, but it is recommended that it be done in a simple setting (GIRM 68).

Supplementary Songs have no specified texts nor are they mandatory. They may accompany a procession or other liturgical action. These include the song during the Presentation of the Gifts, the psalm or song after Communion (GIRM 164), and the Recessional Song.

The following is a list of references to music found in the *General Instruction of the Roman Missal* (2002).

34	acclamations as outward signs of the people's celebration
35	acclamations as active participation
37	music as ritual act or accompanying ritual action
79	elements of the eucharistic prayer
121	Opening Hymn
126	Glory to God
129	Responsorial Psalm
131–132	Gospel acclamation
137	Sung Profession of Faith
139	Liturgical Song During the Preparation of the Gifts and the Altar
147	Acclamations of the Eucharistic Prayer
151	Acclamation
153	Lamb of God
159	Communion Song
164	Hymn or Canticle of Praise after Communion
366	song may not substitute for chants of Mass, e.g., Lamb of God
367	norms for chants between readings, opening song, song during preparation of gifts, Communion Song

What principles should guide my choices?

Music's chief function is ministerial; it must serve and never dominate (MCW 23). One's choices can best be guided by the famous threefold judgment advocated by "Music in Catholic Worship" in 1972—the musical, liturgical, pastoral judgment [see page 155]. Is the music artistically sound and suited to the sacred liturgy? Does it express the scriptural and liturgical texts correctly and support the liturgical action? Is the music suited to the age, culture, and capacity of the assembly?

Music Suited to the Rites

Happily, in recent decades, framers of Church documents, composers, and publishers have recognized an even more sophisticated criterion. Does the music serve the rite?

The rite itself will give you directions for selecting music. (Remember the ten principles in chapter 1? Always begin with the rite!) For example, in the Rite of Ordination of a Priest, Psalm 110 is chosen. It includes the verse, "You are a priest forever like Melchizedeck of old." Nearly every rite will list appropriate acclamations, psalmody, and hymns which bear the weight of tradition and which invite the participation of the assembly.

Newer hymnals now categorize their offerings according to the Church's rites. Most begin with settings for the Hours—Morning Prayer, Evening Prayer, and Night Prayer. Hymnals will also include acclamations and psalmody for the rites of Christian Initiation. In addition, hymns have been sorted into sections with such titles as "Gathering," "Advent," "Christmas," "Lent," "Easter," "Eucharist," and "Mission." Peruse these resources for a clearer understanding of the breadth and scope of the selection process and an appreciation of the need to wed our music to liturgy, not decorate our liturgy with song.

Herein, this author cannot offer a worthy treatment of the role of music in the liturgy nor adequate criteria for its selection. I strongly recommend any of the books that follow so that you may better appreciate the role of music in the liturgy.

FOR FURTHER READING

Archdiocese of Milwaukee. *The Milwaukee Symposium for Church Composers: A Ten Year Report.* Washington, D.C.: The Pastoral Press and Archdiocese of Chicago: Liturgy Training Publications, 1992.

Deiss, Lucien. *Visions of Liturgy and Music for a New Century.* Collegeville: The Liturgical Press, 1996.

Foley, Edward J. *Ritual Music: Studies in Liturgical Musicology.* Beltsville, Md.: The Pastoral Press, 1995 [especially chapters 5 and 6].

Foley, Edward and Mary McGann. *Music and the Eucharistic Prayer.* Collegeville: The Liturgical Press, 1988.

Haas, David. *Music and the Mass.* Archdiocese of Chicago: Liturgy Training Publications, 1998.

Joncas, Jan Michael. *From Sacred Song to Ritual Music: Twentieth Century Understandings of Roman Catholic Worship Music.* Collegeville: The Liturgical Press, 1997.

The Snowbird Statement on Catholic Liturgical Music. Salt Lake City: The Madeleine Institute, 1995.

USCCB. *BCL Newsletter,* Volume XXIX (August/September 1993) 29–34.

Chapter VII

Preparing Parish Liturgies: Sundays, Seasons, Annual Celebrations, Sacramental Rites

Now comes the advice on how to put all this knowledge into practice! Since the preceding chapters have served to establish a firm foundation, each liturgical celebration will be treated here quite succinctly—you will find references to rites, orations, readings, and documents. These will enable you to confidently access pertinent resources.

Always look at a single liturgical season as a whole entity. For example, Advent is a season of joyful expectation. It begins where the season of Ordinary Time concluded, with an admonition to "be prepared" for the coming of the Lord. In the pages of the Lectionary, the Church turns to the Old Testament prophets who anticipated the coming of the Lord. We encounter another prophet, John the Baptist, who heralds the coming of the Messiah. More proximate to Christmas, we find Gospel stories of Mary and Joseph and read of events leading up to the birth in Bethlehem. Even the proper prefaces provide deep theological insights. The orations, readings, and "O" antiphons that we use on the weekdays of Advent from 17 to 24 December especially heighten our anticipation for the coming of the Lord—his historic coming, his coming into our lives every day, and his Second Coming.

One cannot prepare a single celebration in a liturgical season without appreciating all of the celebrations of the season. You might begin with the Lectionary. It provides the thread which weaves this rich tapestry together.

To assist you in preparing for the liturgical seasons, I offer user-friendly charts that provide an overview of possible or mandatory selections; these contain scriptural citations, proper prefaces, and proper blessings. Lectionary numbers, not page numbers, will always be used. Since parishes have purchased Sacramentaries from a variety of publishers, it is difficult to use page numbers.

> Among all who are involved with regard to the rites, pastoral aspects, and music there should be harmony and diligence in the effective preparation of each liturgical celebration in accord with the Missal and other liturgical books. This should take place under the direction of the rector of the church and after consultation with the faithful about things that directly pertain to them . . . (GIRM 111).

SUNDAYS

By a tradition handed down from the apostles and having its origin from the very day of Christ's resurrection, the Church celebrates the paschal mystery every eighth day, which, with good reason, bears the name of the Lord's Day or Sunday. For on this day Christ's faithful must gather together so that, by hearing the word of God and taking part in the eucharist, they may call to mind the passion, the resurrection, and the glorification of the Lord Jesus and may thank God, who "has begotten them unto a living hope through the resurrection of Jesus Christ from the dead" (1 Pt 1:3). Hence the Lord's Day is the first holy day of all and should be proposed to the devotion of the faithful and taught to them in such a way that it may become in fact a day of joy and freedom from work. Other celebrations, unless they be of truly great importance, shall not have precedence over the Sunday, the foundation and core of the whole liturgical year (SC 106).

Dies Domini: On Keeping the Lord's Day Holy by Pope John Paul II (May 31, 1998)

Gather Faithfully Together, Roger Cardinal Mahoney, Archdiocese of Los Angeles

Novo Millennio by John Paul II (1-6-01) section on the Sunday Eucharist, nos. 35–36

Sunday Liturgy Can be Better, Bishop Kenneth Untener, Diocese of Saginaw

Lectionary	Proper of Seasons
Sacramentary	Proper of Seasons
SC	42, 49, 106, 131
Order of Precedence	GNLYC 1, 4, 5, 6, 7, 59
Choices for Sunday	GIRM 53, 113, 115, 354, 357
Weekly Easter	GNLYC 1, 4; DD 1–3, 8, 19–20, 32–33; PS 11, 23, 28–34, 101
Meaning/Importance of	CB 228; DD 27–58, 69–85; PGR 105–108
Role of the Assembly	FYH 1–11
Obligation to attend Mass	SC 106; DD 46–49; DE 115; GFT 80, 88–100
Sunday Readings	LMI 49–57, 66–68, 93, 95, 97, 100, 105, 106, 107
Homily Required	SC 52; GIRM 66; Lectionary #25
The relationship between Easter and Sunday	SC 102, 131; DD 1–3, 8, 19–20, 32–33

ANNUAL CELEBRATIONS: PROPER OF SEASONS

Within the cycle of the year . . . the Church unfolds the whole mystery of Christ, from his incarnation and birth until his ascension, the day of Pentecost, and the expectation of blessed hope and of the Lord's return. Recalling thus the mysteries of redemption the Church opens up to the faithful the riches of the Lord's powers and merits, so that these are in some way made present in every age in order that the faithful may lay hold on them and be filled with saving grace (SC 102).

Advent

Advent has a two-fold character: as a season to prepare for Christmas when Christ's first coming to us is remembered; and as a season when that remembrance directs the mind and hearts to await Christ's Second Coming at the end of time. Advent is thus a period of devout and joyful expectation (GNLYC 39).

In General	GNLYC 39–42; LMI 93–94; CB 235
Vestments	GIRM 336
Choice of Mass	GIRM 353–355; GMEF 11–15
Liturgy of the Hours	GILH 130–133, 147
Blessing of Advent Wreath	BB Chapter 47

Christmas Season

Next to the yearly celebration of the paschal mystery, the Church holds most sacred the memorial of Christ's birth and early manifestations. This is the purpose of the Christmas season (GNLYC 32).

In General	GNLYC 32–38, 39–42; LMI 93–94, 95–96; CB 234; GIRM 346, 354, 355a, b
Liturgy of the Hours	GILH 130, 134, 215, 216
Vigil, Midnight, At Dawn, During the Day	GNLYC 34
The Octave	GNLYC 35
Holy Family	GNLYC 35a
Epiphany	GNLYC 37
Baptism of the Lord	GNLYC 38

Alleluias Advent until December 16	Lectionary #192
Alleluias December 17–24	Lectionary #201 ("O" Antiphons)
Alleluias Christmas Season	Lectionary #211
Alleluias, Weekdays after Epiphany	Lectionary #218

Blessing of Nativity Scene	BB Chapter 48
Blessing of Christmas Tree	BB Chapter 49
Blessing of Homes	BB Chapter 50

Day	Lectionary A B C	Weekday Lectionary #	Preface #	Solemn Blessing
Advent I	1 2 3	175–180	1	1
Advent II	4 5 6	181–186	1	1
Immaculate Conception	6 8 9		58	15
Advent III	7 8 9	187–191	1 or 2	1
Advent IV	10 11 12	(Dec 17–24) 193–200	2	1
Christmas				
(1) Vigil	13	3–5	2	
(2) At Midnight	14	3–5	2	
(3) At Dawn	15	3–5	2	
(4) During Day	16	3–5	2	
Holy Family	17		3–5	S or POP
Mary, Mother of God	18		56	S or 3
Second Sunday of Christmas	19		3–5	S
Epiphany	20		6	4
Baptism of the Lord	21		7	S
Weekdays of Christmas Season		202–218	3–5, 6	S

Lent

Lent is marked by two themes, the baptismal and penitential. By recalling or preparing for baptism and by repentance, this season disposes the faithful, as they more diligently listen to the word of God and devote themselves to prayer, to celebrate the paschal mystery. The baptismal and penitential aspects of Lent are given greater prominence in both the liturgy and liturgical catechesis (SC 109).

Lent, In General	GNLYC 27–31; PS 6–26; CB 253
Vestments	GIRM 346b, d
Music of Lent	PS 18–19, 29, 42, 50, 61, 69–70, 86–87, 91
Ash Wednesday	GNLYC 16, 28–29; CB 253; PS 21–22; GMEF 17
The Sundays of Lent	GNLYC 30; Lectionary #97
Weekdays of Lent	LMI 98 Optional Masses III, IV, V Prefaces #10, 11 Week I to IV Preface #17 Week V
Verses before Gospel	Lectionary #223; GNLYC 28
Holy Week	GNLYC 31; PS 27–37; GMEF 21–25, 28; PGR 23
Passion/Palm Sunday	GNLYC 30–31; CB 263; PS 28–34; GMEF 21–25; BLS 81
Chrism Mass	GNLYC 31a; CB 274; PS 35–36
Catechumenate	LMI 97; CB 249, 253, 260
Rite of Election	RCIA 118–137 or 547–561
Scrutinies	RCIA 150–177
Penitential Rite	RCIA 459–472
Presentations	RCIA 147–149, 157–163, 178–196

Day	Lectionary A B C	Weekday Lectionary #	Preface #	Blessing
Ash Wednesday		219	11	of Ashes BB 52
Thursday		220	8–11	
Friday		221	8–11	
Saturday		222	8–11	
Lent I	22 24 25	224–229	8, 9, 12	POP
Lent II	25 26 27	230–235	8, 9, 13	POP
Lent III	28 29 30	236–242	14 (A) 8, 9	POP
Lent IV	31 32 33	243–249	15 (A) 8, 9	POP
Lent V	34 35 36	250–256	16 (A) 8, 9	POP
Palm Sunday	37, 38		19	5
Monday of HW		257	18	
Tuesday of HW		258	18	
Wednesday of HW		259	18	
Chrism Mass		260	20	

The Easter Triduum

The greatest mysteries of the redemption are celebrated yearly by the church, beginning with the evening Mass of the Lord's Supper on Holy Thursday and ending with Vespers on Easter Sunday. This time is called "the triduum of the crucified, buried and risen"; it is also called the "Easter triduum" because during it is celebrated the paschal mystery, that is, the passing of the Lord from this world to his Father. The church, by the celebration of this mystery through liturgical signs and sacramentals, is united to Christ, her spouse, in intimate communion (PS 38).

In General	LMI 99; PS 38–43; GNLYC 18–21; CB 295, 297, 312, 332, 371; BLS 82–84
Holy Thursday—Evening Mass of the Lord's Supper	PS 44–57; GNLYC 19, 28
Good Friday—Passion of of Our Lord	PS 58–72; CB 312; GNLYC 20
Holy Saturday	PS 73–76; GNLYC 20; RCIA 185–205; BB Chapter 54
Easter Vigil	PS 77–96; Lectionary #99; GNLYC 17–21; CB 332; PS 3, 77–96, GILH 70
Easter Sunday	PS 97–99
Liturgy of the Hours	GILH 68, 70, 82, 130, 133, 134, 151, 152, 208–214; CB 371

Day	Lectionary ABC	Preface #	Solemn Blessing	Comments
Evening Mass of Lord's Supper	39	P 47	None	Transfer of the Holy Eucharist
Good Friday of the Lord's Passion	40		Special Blessing	Liturgy of Word with Solemn Intercesssions. Veneration of the Cross. Holy Communion.
Easter Vigil	41	P 21	6	Rites of Initiation
Easter Day	42	P 21	6 Double Alleluia at Dismissal	Renewal of Baptismal Promises

The Easter Season

The fifty days from Easter Sunday to Pentecost are celebrated in joyful exultation as one feast day, or better as one "great Sunday" (GNLYC 22).

In General	GNLYC 22–26; PS 100–108; CB 371; LMI 99–102; GMEF 1–29
Easter and Sunday	SC 102, 131; DD 1–3, 8, 19–20, 32–33
The Octave	GNLYC 24; double alleluias GILH
The Sundays of Easter	GNLYC 23
Weekdays	GNLYC 26
Alleluias	Double alleluias during Octave at dismissal Easter to Ascension Lectionary #303 Ascension to Pentecost Lectionary #304
Prefaces	#26 and 27
Ascension	GNLYC 25; LMI 102 Lectionary #58; when Ascension is moved to the Seventh Sunday of Easter, use Lectionary #294 for Thursday of Sixth Week of Easter
Pentecost	GNLYC 22, 26; LMI 102; DD 20, 28, 76; PS 103–107; IRL 13; GMEF 2

Liturgy of the Hours   GILH 152, 214

Mystagogia   RCIA 244–251

Day	Lectionary A B C	Weekday Lectionary #	Preface #	Blessing
Octave of Easter				
Monday	261		21	Double
Tuesday	262		21	Alleluia
Wednesday	263		21	in Dismissal
Thursday	264		21	
Friday	265		21	Blessing 6 or
Saturday	266		21	Special POP
Easter II	43 44 45	267–272	21, 22–25	7
Easter III	46 47 48	273–278	21, 22–25	7
Easter IV	49 50 51	279–284	21, 22–25	7
Easter V	52 53 54	285–290	21, 22–25	7
Easter VI	55 56 57	291–296	21, 22–25	7
Ascension	58		26	8
Easter VII	59 60 61	297–302	21, 22–25	7
Pentecost				
Vigil	62		28	9
Day	63		28	9

ORDINARY TIME

Apart from those seasons having their own distinctive character, thirty-three or thirty-four weeks remain in the yearly cycle that do not celebrate a specific aspect of the mystery of Christ. Rather, especially on the Sundays, they are devoted to the mystery of Christ in all its aspects. This period is known as Ordinary Time (GNLYC 43).

In General   GNLYC 16, 43–44

Sundays   LMI 103–107

Weekdays   LMI 109–110; GIRM 346c, 355c, 363, 377

Alleluias   Sundays of Ordinary Time, Lectionary #163
                 Weekdays of the Year, Lectionary #509

Sunday Prefaces   #29–36

Weekday Prefaces   #37–42

BVM on Saturday   GNLYC 15; GIRM 378

Sunday in Ordinary Time	Lectionary A	B	C	Weekday Lectionary #	Preface #	Blessing (or POP)
1 Baptism of Lord		21		305–310	7	P over P #7
2	64	65	66	311–316	29–36; 37–42	10–14
3	67	68	69	317–322	29–36; 37–42	10–14
4	70	71	72	323–328	29–36; 37–42	10–14
5	73	74	75	329–334	29–36; 37–42	10–14
6	76	77	78	335–340	29–36; 37–42	10–14
7	79	80	81	341–346	29–36; 37–42	10–14
8	82	83	84	347–352	29–36; 37–42	10–14
9	85	86	87	353–358	29–36; 37–42	10–14
10	88	89	90	359–364	29–36; 37–42	10–14
11	91	92	93	365–370	29–36; 37–42	10–14
12	94	95	96	371–376	29–36; 37–42	10–14
13	97	98	99	377–382	29–36; 37–42	10–14
14	100	101	102	383–388	29–36; 37–42	10–14
15	103	104	105	389–394	29–36; 37–42	10–14
16	106	107	108	395–400	29–36; 37–42	10–14
17	109	110	111	401–406	29–36; 37–42	10–14
18	112	113	114	407–412	29–36; 37–42	10–14
19	115	116	117	413–418	29–36; 37–42	10–14
20	118	119	120	419–424	29–36; 37–42	10–14
21	121	122	123	425–430	29–36; 37–42	10–14
22	124	125	126	431–436	29–36; 37–42	10–14
23	127	128	129	437–442	29–36; 37–42	10–14
24	130	131	132	443–448	29–36; 37–42	10–14
25	133	134	135	449–454	29–36; 37–42	10–14
26	136	137	138	455–460	29–36; 37–42	10–14
27	139	140	141	461–466	29–36; 37–42	10–14
28	142	143	144	467–472	29–36; 37–42	10–14
29	145	146	147	473–478	29–36; 37–42	10–14
30	148	149	150	479–484	29–36; 37–42	10–14
31	151	152	153	485–490	29–36; 37–42	10–14
32	154	155	156	491–496	29–36; 37–42	10–14
33	157	158	159	497–502	29–36; 37–42	10–14
34 Christ the King	160	161	162	503–508	51	10–14

SOLEMNITIES AND FEASTS

As it celebrates the mystery of Christ in yearly cycle, the Church also venerates with a particular love Mary, the Mother of God, and sets before the devotion of the faithful the memory of the martyrs and other saints (GNLYC 8).

According to their importance, celebrations are distinguished from each other and named as follows: solemnities, feasts, memorials (GNLYC 10).

DAY	DATE	RANK	LECTIONARY A B C	ORATIONS	PREFACE #
Most Holy Trinity	Sunday after Pentecost	S	164 165 166	propers	43
Body & Blood of Christ	2nd Sunday after Pent.	S	167 168 169	propers	48
Sacred Heart	Fri. after B&B	F	170 171 172	propers	45
Immaculate Heart of Mary	Sat. after 2nd Sunday after Pentecost	F	707–712	propers	56, 57
Presentation	February 2	F	524	propers	49
Joseph, Husband of Mary *	March 19	S	543	propers	62
Annunciation	March 25	S	545	propers	44
John the Baptist Vigil Day	June 24	S	586 587	propers propers	61
Peter and Paul Vigil Day	June 29	S	590 591	propers propers	63
Transfiguration	August 6	F	614	propers	50
Assumption Vigil Day	August 15	S	621 622	propers propers	59
Triumph of the Cross	Sept. 14	F	638	propers	46 *(cont'd)*

(continued) DAY	DATE	RANK	LECTIONARY A B C	ORATIONS	PREFACE #
All Saints	November 1	S	667	propers	71
All Souls	November 2		668	propers (3)	77–81
Dedication of the Lateran Basilica	November 9	F	671	Common. Dedication of Church	52, 53
Christ the King	Last Sun OT	S	161 162 163	propers	51
Immac. Conc. of BVM	December 8	S	689	propers	58
Dedication/ Anniversary	Varies	S	701–706	Anniv. of Dedication	52, 53

*Blessing of Food for St. Joseph's Table (March 19) BB Chapter 53

In General GNLYC 8–15; LMI 108; GILH 71, 73, 117, 119, 134, 199, 225–236

HOLY DAYS OF OBLIGATION

There are six holy days of obligation in the United States—The Immaculate Conception (December 8), The Nativity of the Lord/Christmas (December 25), Mary, Mother of God (January 1), Ascension of the Lord (varies), Assumption of the BVM (August 15), and All Saints (November 1).

In November 1992, the United States bishops decided that whenever the solemnities of Mary, Mother of God, the Assumption, or All Saints fell on a Saturday or Monday, the obligation to attend Mass was abrogated. This was approved by Rome and the decision became effective on January 1, 1993. This applies to these three days *only*.

Christmas and the Immaculate Conception are never affected by this decision. The latter is the patronal feast of the United States. The solemnity of the Ascension usually fell on a Thursday, but has recently been moved to the Seventh Sunday of Easter in most dioceses of the United States.

The Sanctoral Cycle SC 111; GNLYC 8–15; LMI 70, 71, 83, 84

Lectionary	Proper of the Saints	#510–700
	The Common of the BVM	#707–712
	The Common of the Martyrs	#713–718
	The Common of Pastors	#719–724
	The Common of Doctors of the Church	#725–730
	The Common of Virgins	#731–736
	The Common of Holy Men and Women	#737–742

Sacramentary	Proper of the Saints
	The Common of the BVM
	The Common of the Martyrs
	The Common of Pastors
	The Common of Doctors of the Church
	The Common of Virgins
	The Common of Holy Men and Women

GILH   71, 117, 118, 119, 116, 199, 218–224

GIRM   375, 378

LITURGY OF THE HOURS

Public and common prayer by the people of God is rightly considered to be among the primary duties of the Church. From the very beginning those who were baptized "devoted themselves to the teaching of the apostles and to the community, to the breaking of the bread, and to prayer" (Acts 2:42). The acts of the Apostles give frequent testimony to the fact that the Christian community prayed with one accord. The witness of the early Church teaches us that individual Christians devoted themselves to prayer at fixed times. Then, in different places, it soon became the established practice to assign special times for common prayer, for example, the last hour of the day when evening draws on and the lamp is lighted, or the first hour when night draws to a close with the rising of the sun. . . . Such prayer in common gradually took the form of a set cycle of hours. This liturgy of the hours or divine office, enriched by readings, is principally a prayer of praise and petition. Indeed, it is the prayer of the Church with Christ and to Christ (GILH 1, 2).

Importance of	SC 84, 88; IRL 61; GILH 1–33
Component hours	SC 88, 94; GNLYC 3; GILH 34–99 Office of Readings Morning Prayer Midday Prayer Evening Prayer [Solemn Vespers] Night Prayer
Elements of	SC 83–85, 90; DD 27; GILH 100–283
Psalms and Canticles	GILH 126–139; [see charts, Appendix]
Various Seasons	GILH Chapter IV
Celebration	SC 89–101; GILH 202–252; 253–284; BLS 115
Celebration in Common	GILH 253–284
Combining with Mass	GILH 93–99
Music	SC 93, 99; GILH 121–125; LMT 34–45

See Appendix for planning sheets for Morning Prayer, Evening Prayer, and Night Prayer.

FOR FURTHER READING

Bishops' Committee on the Liturgy. *Liturgy of the Hours, Study Text VII.* Washington, D.C.: USCCB, 1981.

Bradshaw, Paul F. *Two Ways of Praying.* Nashville: Abingdon Press, 1995.

"General Instruction of the Liturgy of the Hours" (1971), as found in *The Liturgy Documents, Volume II,* 260–313. Chicago: Liturgy Training Publications, 1999.

Miller, Charles. *Together in Prayer: Learning to Love the Liturgy of the Hours.* New York: Alba House, 1994.

Richards, James. *Preparing Morning Prayer and Evening Prayer.* Collegeville: The Liturgical Press, 1997.

Taft, Robert. *The Liturgy of the Hours in East and West.* Collegeville: The Liturgical Press, 1986.

Video—*Praying at All Times.* San Diego: Diocese of San Diego, 2000 (24 minutes).

Zimmerman, Joyce Ann. *Morning and Evening Prayer: A Parish Celebration.* Archdiocese of Chicago: Liturgy Training Publications, 1996.

SACRAMENTAL CELEBRATIONS

The purpose of the sacraments is to make people holy, to build up the Body of Christ, and, finally, to give worship to God; but being signs they also have a teaching function. They do not presuppose faith, but by words and objects they also nourish, strengthen, and express it; that is why they are called "sacraments of faith." They do indeed impart grace, but in addition, the very act of celebrating them disposes the faithful most effectively to receive this grace in a fruitful manner, to worship God rightly, and to practice charity.

It is therefore of the highest importance that the faithful should readily understand the sacramental signs and should with great eagerness frequent those sacraments that were instituted to nourish the Christian life (SC 59).

Those who prepare sacramental celebrations have a great obligation to understand them more fully. For an outline and description of each rite, please consult chapter II of this book. Here, you will find succinct references to the rite itself, Sacramentary and Lectionary citations, and complementary resources. Finally, please turn to the Appendix to find worksheets designed to make collaborative planning much easier and productive.

The Rite of Baptism for Children

From the earliest times, the Church, to which the mission of the preaching of the Gospel and of baptizing was entrusted, has baptized not only adults but children as well. Our Lord said: "Unless a man is reborn in water and the Holy Spirit, he cannot enter the kingdom of God." The Church has understood these words to mean that children should not be deprived of baptism, because they are baptized in the faith of the Church, a faith proclaimed for them by their parents and godparents, who represent both the local Church and the whole society of saints and believers: "The whole Church is the mother of all and the mother of each" (RBC 2).

In general, one must understand that this is not a "private" event for the family. At least part of the parish community should be present (RBC 4). If at all possible, this rite should be celebrated within Sunday Mass. Parents and godparents serve a vital role in this ritual (RBC 5, 6) and it is assumed that they have attended preparation classes at the parish before the ceremony (RBC 7).

Members of the community might sew a white garment; some families may have an heirloom gown which is used at each baptism. In either case, it is best that it not be worn to Church but that the child be dressed in it during the explanatory rites.

In General	CIGI 1–6; RBC 1–3; SC 6, 67–70; DANE IV
Day and Place	RBC 8–14; Easter Sunday, Pentecost, any day
Font	SC 128; CB 52; BLS 66–69
Proper Ministers	RBC 4–7
Music	MCW 80; LMT 8, 22–26
Readings	RBC 186–215, Mass of the Day, or Lectionary #756–760
Sacramentary	Mass of the Day or Ritual Mass, Christian Initiation: Baptism

The Rite of Baptism—Within, Outside of Mass

For Several Children	#32–71
For One Child	#72–106
For a Large Number of Children	#107–131
Rite of Baptism for Children Administered by a Catechist	#132–156
For Children in Danger of Death, No Priest or Deacon Present	#157–164
Rite of Bringing a Baptized Child to Church	#165–185

The Rite of Christian Initiation of Adults

The initiation of Catechumens is a gradual process that takes place within the community of the faithful. By joining the catechumens in reflecting on the value of the paschal mystery and by renewing their own conversion, the faithful provide an example that will help the catechumens to obey the Holy Spirit more generously (RCIA 4).

Theology of the Rites	CIGI 1–6; RCIA 1–8; *praenotanda* of each rite
In General	SC 64–71; IRL 56; GSPD 8–13
Ministries	
Bishop	RCIA 12, 121, 207, 247–248, 251, 548
Priest	RCIA 13, 14, 45, 98, 106–111, 145, 247–248, 308, 331–335, 448, 562–565
Deacon	RCIA 15, 45, 98, 145
Catechist	RCIA 16, 81–89, 91, 96, 160, 180
Faithful/Team	RCIA 4, 9
Sponsors/Godparents	RCIA 10, 11

Time and Place   RCIA 8, 17–30; SC 14; DD 25–41; GNLYC 27;
                            CB 249; PS 6–10, 88–89, 102, 103

Church Building   BLS 66–69, 101, 117

Music   MCW 80; LMT 8, 22–26; RCIA Appendix II

Mystagogia   RCIA 244–251

Law   National Statutes on the Catechumenate
                            1–37; CIC 206, 787–789, 842, 851, 852, 863,
                            865, 866, 869, 883, 884, 885, 1170, 1183

The Rites of Initiation and Full Reception into Communion		
CATECHUMENS	CANDIDATES	COMBINED RITES (USA)
Rite of Acceptance into the Order of Catechumens RCIA 41–74; LM #743	Rite of Welcoming the Candidates RCIA 411–433	Rite of Acceptance into the Order of Catechumens and the Rite of Welcoming Baptized but Previously Uncatechized Adults Who Are Preparing for Confirm and/or Eucharist or Reception into the Full Communion of the Catholic Church RCIA 505–529
Celebration of the Word RCIA 81–89		
Minor Exorcisms RCIA 90–94		
Blessings of the Catechumens RCIA 95–97		
Anointing of the Catechumens RCIA 98–101		
Presentation of the Creed Third Week of Lent RCIA 147–148 and 157–163; LM #748		

Presentation of the Lord's Prayer Fifth Week of Lent RCIA 147, 149, and 178–196; LM #749–750		
Sending of the Catechumens for Election RCIA 106–117	Rite of Sending the Candidates for Recognition by the Bishop and for the Call to Continuing Conversion RCIA 434–445	Parish Celebration for Sending Catechumens for Election and Candidates for Recognition by the Bishop RCIA 530–546
Rite of Election or Enrollment of Names RCIA 118–137; LM #22–24, 744	Rite of Calling the Candidates to Continuing Conversion RCIA 446–458	Celebration of the Rite of Election for Catechumens and of the Call to Continuing Conversion of Candidates Who Are Preparing for Confirmation and/or Eucharist or Reception into Full Communion of the Catholic Church RCIA 547–561
First Scrutiny (Lent III) RCIA 150-156; LM #745, 28 Second Scrutiny (Lent IV) RCIA 164–170; LM #746, 31	Penitential Rite (Second Sunday of Lent) RCIA 459–472	
Third Scrutiny (Lent V) RCIA 171–177; LM #747, 34		
Preparation Rites of Holy Saturday RCIA 185–199; LM #750		
Celebration of the Sacraments of Initiation RCIA 206–243; LM #751–755, 41	Reception of Baptized Christians into the Full Communion of the Catholic Church within Mass/outside Mass RCIA 473–504; LM #761–763	Celebration at the Easter Vigil of the Sacraments of Initiation and of the Rite of Reception into the Full Communion of the Catholic Church RCIA 562–594

> ## The Initiation of Children of Catechetical Age
>
> This form of the rite of Christian initiation is intended for children, not baptized as infants, who have attained the use of reason and are of catechetical age. They seek Christian initiation either at the direction of their parents or guardians or, with parental permission, on their own initiative. Such children are capable of receiving and nurturing a personal faith and of recognizing an obligation in conscience. But they cannot yet be treated as adults because, at this stage in their lives, they are dependent on their parents or guardians and are still strongly influenced by their companions and social surroundings (RCIA 252).

Catechesis   RCIA 253, 254, 255

Sponsors,
Godparents   SC 67; CIC 872, 873, 874

Celebrations   256, 257, 258, 259, *praenotanda* for each rite
                    RCIA Part II, Section I   (252–330)
                    Acceptance into the Order of Catechumens   (260–276)
                    Rite of Election and Enrollment of Names   (277–290)
                    Scrutinies   (291–303)
                    Sacraments of Initiation   (304–329)
                    Period of Postbaptismal Catechesis or
                        Mystagogy   (330)
                    Cf. *Directory for Masses with Children*

Lectionary   Entrance into the Order of Catechumens   743
                    Election   744, 22–24
                    Scrutinies   745–747
                    Presentation of the Creed   748
                    Presentation of the Lord's Prayer   749–750
                    Initiation Apart from Easter Vigil   751–755

Law   National Statutes #18–19

The Initiation of Adults in Exceptional Circumstances

The extraordinary circumstances in question are either events that prevent the candidate from completing all the steps of the Catechumenate or a depth of Christian conversion and a degree of religious maturity that lead the local bishop to decide that the candidate may receive baptism without delay (RCIA 331).

See RCIA Part II, no. 2

Introduction   RCIA 331–339

Rite   RCIA 340–369

Initiation of Persons in Danger of Death

Persons, whether catechumens or not, who are in danger of death but are not at the point of death and so are able to hear and answer the questions involved may be baptized with this short rite (RCIA 370).

See RCIA Part II, no. 3

Introduction   RCIA 370–374

Rite   RCIA 375–399

Uncatechized Adult Catholics Preparing for Confirmation and Eucharist

Concerns adults who were baptized as infants either as Roman Catholics or as members of another Christian community but did not receive further catechetical formation nor, consequently, the sacraments of confirmation or eucharist . . . (RCIA 400).

See RCIA Part II, no. 4

Optional Rites
    Welcoming the Candidates   RCIA 411–433
    Rite of Sending for Recognition
      by Bishop   RCIA 434–445
    Rite of Calling the Candidates
      to Continuing Conversion   RCIA 446–458
    Penitential Rite   RCIA 459–472

Lectionary   #761–763, 764–768

Law   National Statutes #25–29

**Reception of Baptized Christians
into the Full Communion of the Catholic Church**

This is the liturgical rite by which a person born and baptized in a separated ecclesial Community is received, according to the Latin rite, into the full communion of the Catholic Church. The Rite is so arranged that no greater burden than necessary (see Acts 15:28) is required for the establishment of communion and unity (RCIA 473).

In the case of Eastern Christians who enter into the fullness of Catholic communion, no liturgical rite is required, but simply a profession of Catholic faith, even if such persons are permitted, in virtue of recourse to the Apostolic See, to transfer to the Latin rite (RCIA 474).

RCIA Part II, nos. 4 and 5

In General	RCIA 473–486; GIRM 372

Candidates for Reception into Full Communion

Rite of Welcome	RCIA 411–433
Rite of Sending	RCIA 434–445
Call to Continuing Conversion	RCIA 446–458
Penitential Rite	RCIA 459–472
Reception into Full Communion	
Introduction	RCIA 473–486
Within Mass	RCIA 487–498
Outside Mass	RCIA 499–504
Readings	Lectionary #761–763, 867–871, or Mass of Day

See also the combined rites	RCIA: USA Appendix
Acceptance/Welcome	RCIA 505–529
Sending Catechumens for Election/Candidates for Recognition	RCIA 530–546
Rite of Election/Call to Continuing Conversion	RCIA 547–561
Celebration at the Easter Vigil— Initiation/Reception	RCIA 562–594

Law	National Statutes #30–37

The Rite of Confirmation

Those who have been baptized continue on the path of Christian Initiation through the sacrament of confirmation. In this sacrament they receive the Holy Spirit whom the Lord sent upon the apostles on Pentecost. This giving of the Holy Spirit conforms believers more fully to Christ and strengthens them so that they may bear witness to Christ for the building up of his Body in faith and love. They are so marked with the character or seal of the Lord that the sacrament of confirmation cannot be repeated (RC nos. 1, 2).

In General	RC 1–19; SC 71; CB 1182; GSPD 14–18; DE 99, 101
Rite of Confirmation	
Within Mass	RC 20–33
Readings	Mass of the Day; Lectionary #763–767; RC 57–65
Preface of Day	
or Preface of	
the Holy Spirit	Preface #54, 55
Ritual Mass:	
Initiation:	
Confirmation	Propers, Solemn Blessing, POP
Vestments	GIRM 347
Rite of Confirmation	
Outside Mass	RC 34–49
When a Pastor	RC 50–51 Rite of Confirmation by a Minister
Presides	Who Is Not a Bishop
Confirmation in	
Danger of Death	RC 52–56
Music	MCW 82; LMT 8

Contact your Office of Worship to see if there are diocesan guidelines for the celebration of this sacrament. Your bishop may have specific requests regarding the confirmation liturgies in his diocese.

Solemn First Communion

At the table of the eucharist, we eat the flesh and drink the blood of the Son of Man so that we may have eternal life and show forth the unity of God's people. By offering ourselves with Christ, we share in the universal sacrifice, that is, the entire community of the redeemed offered to God by their High Priest and we pray for a greater outpouring of the Holy Spirit, so that the whole human race may be brought into the unity of God's family (CIGI 2).

Preparation of the Liturgy	DMC 29
Liturgical Catechesis for First Communion	DMC 12; 1–8, 8–15
Meaning of the Sacrament	SC 6, 47; DMC 8–15; CB 297; GMEF 3
Paschal Mystery	SC 5–9, 106; GNLYC 1, 4, 18–21; LMT 46

The Choice of Mass and Its Parts

Readings	Lectionary #769; DMC 40–47
Mass of the Day	Varies
Votive Mass:	
Holy Eucharist	Lectionary #904–909
Eucharistic Prayer	Preface #47 or 48 (Holy Eucharist)
	Proper Preface of Day
Eucharistic Prayers for Children	C1, C2, C3 (their own preface)
Office and Ministries in the Celebration	DMC 22–24
Procession	DMC 34
Music	DMC 30–32, 48, 62, 72; LMT 18
Gestures	DMC 33–34
Bread	GIRM 319–324

> **Pastoral Care of the Sick: Rites of Anointing and Viaticum**
>
> The Lord himself showed great concern for the bodily and spiritual welfare of the sick and commanded his followers to do likewise. This is clear from the gospels, and above all from the existence of the sacrament of anointing, which he instituted and which is made known in the letter of James. Since then the Church has never failed to celebrate this sacrament for its members by the anointing and the prayer of its priests, commending those who are ill to the suffering and glorified Lord, that he may raise them up and save them (James 5:14-16). Moreover, the Church exhorts them to associate themselves willingly with the passion and death of Christ (Romans 8:17) and thus contribute to the welfare of the people of God (PCS:GI 5).
>
> The rites of Part II . . . are used by the Church to comfort and strengthen a dying Christian in the passage from this life. The ministry to the dying places emphasis on trust in the Lord's promise of eternal life rather than on the struggle against illness which is characteristic of the pastoral care of the sick (PCS 161).

This liturgical book should be read and used carefully. It clearly distinguishes between two pastoral practices—comforting the sick and ministering to the dying. These are segregated into parts one and two of the rite book. Moreover, the first three chapters of Part II include rites which can be celebrated fully, but the rites in chapter 8, "Rites for Exceptional Circumstances," are to be used in emergency situations.

In light of these pastoral realities, the ICEL translation, used in the USA, includes additions to the *editio typica*. It addresses pastoral circumstances not foreseen in the original or provisional texts and includes excerpts from other parts of the *Roman Ritual—Rite of Funerals, Rite of Christian Initiation of Adults*, and the *Rite of Penance*.

General Introduction (1–41)

I. Pastoral Care of the Sick

Introduction (42–53)

Visits to the Sick (54–61)

Visits to a Sick Child (62–70)

Communion of the Sick (71–80)

    Ordinary Circumstances (81–91)
    In a Hospital or Institution (92–96)

Anointing of the Sick (97–110)

    Outside Mass (111–130)
    Within Mass (131–148)
    In a Hospital or Institution (149–160)

II. Pastoral Care of the Dying

Introduction (161–174)

Celebration of Viaticum (175–188)

    Within Mass (189–196)
    Outside Mass (197–211)

Commendation of the Dying (212–222)

Prayers for the Dead (223–231)

Rites for Exceptional Circumstances (232–235)

    Continuous Rite of Penance, Anointing, and Viaticum (236–258)
    Rites for Emergencies (259–274)
    Christian Initiation for the Dying (275–296)

III. Readings, Responses, and Virtues for Sacred Scripture (297–298)

Appendix: Rite for Reconciliation of Individual Penitents (299–305)
    Biblical Index

In General   SC 73–75, 79; GSPD 26–29; GIRM 368, 372, 379–385; BLS 109

Music   MCW 81

Readings

    For the Anointing of the Sick   Lectionary #790–795
    Viaticum   Lectionary #796–800
    For the Sick   Lectionary #933–937
    For the Grace of a Happy Death   Lectionary #963–967
    PCS 297–298 and Appendix

Sacramentary   Mass for the Sick; Mass for the Grace of a Happy Death

The Sacrament of Reconciliation

The Father has shown forth his mercy by reconciling the world to himself in Christ and by making peace for all things on earth and in heaven by the blood of Christ on the cross. The Son of God made man lived among us in order to free us from the slavery of sin and to call us out of darkness into his wonderful light. He therefore began his work on earth by preaching repentance and saying "Repent and believe the Gospel" (Mark 1:15) (Rite of Penance 1).

The Rites

> Rite of Reconciliation of Individual Penitents (41–42)
> Rite of Reconciliation of Several Penitents with Individual
>   Confession and Absolution (48–59)
> Rite of Reconciliation of Several Penitents with General Confession
>   and Absolution (60–66)
> Appendices
>> Absolution from Censures
>> Sample Penitential Services for Lent and Advent
>> Sample Examination of Conscience

In General   SC 72, 110; BLS 103–105; GSPD 22–25; DD 44

Music   MCW 81; LMT 21, 27

In Lent   PS 9–10, 14–15, 37; CB 253

Readings   see Scripture collection in RP; cf. Lectionary #948–952

Sacramentary   The sacrament of reconciliaton is never celebrated
                within Mass.

Marriage

In virtue of the sacrament of marriage, married Christians signify and share in the mystery of the unity and fruitful love that exists between Christ and his Church; they thus help each other to attain holiness in their married life and in welcoming and rearing children; and they have their own special place among the people of God.

A marriage is established by the marriage covenant, the irrevocable consent that the spouses freely give to and receive from each other. . . . To make the indissoluble marriage covenant a clearer sign of this meaning and a surer help in its fulfillment, Christ the Lord raised it to the dignity of a sacrament, modeled after his own nuptial bond with the Church (Rite of Marriage 1, 2).

In General	SC 77–78; GSPD 34–39; CB 598–600, 601–613, 614–620; BLS 106–108
Preparation	RM 5, 6, 7
Choice of Rite	RM 8
Rite I Between a Catholic and a Catholic	RM 19–38 and Chapters IV and V
Rite II Catholic and Non-Catholic Christian	RM 39–54
Rite III Catholic and a Non-Christian	RM 55–66
Choice of Day	RM 11
Readings	Lectionary #801–805; RM 11
Sacramentary	Ritual Masses: Wedding Mass
Local Customs	RM 12–16
Music	MCW 82; LMT 28–29; diocesan music policies; parish music policies

Sacramental Celebrations 207

Holy Orders

. . . Pour out now upon this chosen one that power which is from you, the Spirit of governance whom you gave to your beloved Son, Jesus Christ, the Spirit who he bestowed upon the holy Apostles who established the Church in each place as your sanctuary for the glory and unceasing praise of your name. Grant, O Father, knower of all hearts, that this your servant whom you have chosen for the office of Bishop may shepherd your holy flock. Serving you night and day, may he fulfill before you without reproach the ministry of the High Priesthood; so that, always gaining your favor, he may offer up the gifts of your holy Church. Grant that by the power of the Spirit of the High Priesthood, he may have the power to forgive sins according to your command, assign offices according to your decree, and loose every bond according to the power given by you to the Apostles . . . *(Prayer of Ordination of a Bishop).*

You will rarely be asked to plan an ordination at your parish. This is conducted in the cathedral or a place of the bishop's designation, such as a seminary. But you may wish to be familiar with the rite, especially if you are to catechize young children about it. Perhaps your parish intern is being ordained as a transitional deacon. For an overview of the *Rite of Ordination*, see chapter III, pages 89–91.

Occasionally, a bishop may celebrate the Rite of Candidacy in a seminarian's home parish. See *Rite of Admission to Candidacy for Ordination as Deacons and Priests.* It may be found in the Appendix of the *Rite of Ordination.*

In General   SC 76; GSPD 30–33

Lectionary

    For the Conferral of Holy Orders #770–774
    Admission to Candidacy   #775–779
    Institution of Readers   #780–784
    Institution of Acolytes   #785–789

Sacramentary   Ritual Mass: Holy Orders

Music   Psalm 110; *Veni Creator Spiritus*

See also Mass for Pope or Bishop, especially on their anniversary (cf. Lectionary #832); Mass for the Election of a Pope or Bishop (cf. Lectionary #833–837); Mass for Priests (cf. Lectionary #843–847); Mass for Ministers of the Church (cf. Lectionary #848–851).

Chapter VIII

More Parish Celebrations

This chapter will address those other rites and Masses that are probably celebrated less frequently in your parish. Once again, these pages supply quick references for those who will prepare the liturgies. You will find worksheets for many of these rites in the Appendix.

LITURGY AND THE CHURCH BUILDING

The church is the proper place for the liturgical prayer of the parish community, especially the celebration of the Eucharist on Sunday. It is also the privileged place for adoration of the Blessed Sacrament and reservation of the Eucharist for Communion to the sick. Whenever communities have built houses for worship, the design of the building has been of critical importance. Churches are never "simply gathering spaces but signify and make visible the Church living in a particular place, the dwelling of God" among us, now "reconciled and united in Christ." As such, the building itself becomes a sign of the pilgrim Church on earth and reflects the Church dwelling in heaven. Every church building is a gathering place for the assembly, a resting place, a place of encounter with God as well as a point of departure on the Church's unfinished journey toward the reign of God (BLS 17; cf. CCC 1691, 1180).

Theological principles

> BLS 12–45; CCC 1180; GIRM 253–254

Building and Renovation

> GIRM Chapter V
> Diocesan and Parish Process—*Built of Living Stones* Chapter IV
> SC 125, 128; GIRM 257; GSPD 1–7
> Re: Renovation of Older Churches BLS 238–256
> Contact your Office of Worship for Diocesan Guidelines

Parts of the Church

Assembly	All, but especially BLS 49–53, 85–87, 95; GIRM 294, 311
Sanctuary	BLS 54–55; GIRM 295
Altar	BLS 56–60; SC 128; GIRM 49, 73, 123, 169, 273, 296–308; CB 48, 72–73; RDCA 2.16, 4.1–4.30
Ambo	BLS 61–62; GIRM 309; LMI 32–34; CB 51
P. Chair	BLS 63–65; GIRM 310
Baptistry	BLS 66–69; SC 128
Reservation of the Eucharist	BLS 70–80; HCWEOM 5–11; GIRM 314–317; EM 51; CIC 938

Vessels	GIRM 327–334; BLS 164–165
Vestments	GIRM 335–347; BLS 164–165

Music BLS 88–90; SC 120; MCW 38; LMT 56–59

Other furnishings BLS 91–94; PS 82, 83, 99; SC 122–128; GIRM 288–295, 310–318, 325–326, 348–351; CB 37–38, 42–54

Decorations BLS 122–129; PS 17, 26

Blessing of Items for Liturgical Use BB Chapters 31–43; RDCA Chapter 7; Lectionary #823–826

DEDICATION OF A CHURCH

Because the church is a visible building, it stands as a special sign of the pilgrim Church on earth and reflects the Church dwelling in heaven. When a church is erected as a building solely and permanently for assembling the people of God and for carrying out sacred functions, it is fitting that it be dedicated to God with a solemn rite, in accord with the ancient custom of the Church (RDCA Chapter 2, #2).

In General

GIRM 290; GNLYC 59
Rite of Dedication of a Church and an Altar
Appendix VIII of Sacramentary

Rites of Dedication and Blessing

Blessing a building site, laying a foundation stone, or commencement of work	RDCA Chapter 1
Dedication of a Church	RDCA Chapter 2
Dedication of a Church Already in General Use	RDCA Chapter 3
Dedication of an Altar	RDCA Chapter 4
Blessing of a Church (chapel or oratory)	RDCA Chapter 5
Blessing of an Altar	RDCA Chapter 6
Blessing of a Chalice and Paten	RDCA Chapter 7; Appendix IX of Sacramentary
Lectionary	#816, 817–822
Sacramentary	Common of a Dedication of a Church; RDCA Chapter II

Anniversary of the Dedication of a Church

GNLYC 59; RDCA Chapter II, 26–27
Lectionary   #701–706
Sacramentary   Common of Dedication of a Church; Preface #52 and 53

FUNERALS

The Church through its funeral rites commends the dead to God's merciful love and pleads for the forgiveness of their sins. At the funeral rites, especially at the celebration of the Eucharistic sacrifice, the Christian Community affirms and expresses the union of the Church on earth with the Church in heaven in the one great communion of saints. Though separated from the living, the dead are still at one with the community of believers on earth and benefit from their prayers and intercessions. At the rite of final commendation and farewell, the community acknowledges the reality of separation and commends the deceased to God. In this way it recognizes the spiritual bond that still exists between the living and the dead and proclaims its belief that all the faithful will be raised up and reunited in the new heavens and a new earth, where death will be no more (OCF:GI #6).

Related Rites and Prayers

OCF 101–108	Prayer after Death
OCF 109–118	Gathering in the Presence of the Body
OCF 119–127	Transfer of the Body to the Church or to the Place of Committal
OCF 54–81	Vigil for the Deceased
OCF 82–97	Vigil for the Deceased with Reception at the Church
OCF 243–263	Vigil for a Deceased Child

Funeral Liturgy

OCF 154–176	Funeral Mass
OCF 264–282	Funeral Mass (for a Child)
OCF 177–203	Funeral Liturgy outside Mass
OCF 295–315	Funeral Liturgy outside Mass (for a Child)
OCF 204–223	Rite of Committal
OCF 316–326	Rite of Committal (for a Child)
OCF 224–233	Rite of Committal with Final Commendation
OCF 327–336	Rite of Committal with Final Commendation (for a Child)
OCF 337–342	Rite of Commendation for an Infant

Texts of Sacred Scripture

OCF 345	Funerals for Adults
OCF 346	Funerals for Baptized Children
OCF 346	Funerals for Children Who Have Died before Baptism

Liturgy of the Hours

OCF 348–372	Office for the Dead
OCF 373–384	Morning Prayer
OCF 385–395	Evening Prayer

Additional Texts   **OCF 397–410**

Sacramentary	Masses for the Dead
Lectionary	#1011–1016; 1017–1022; 1023–1026
Book of Blessings	Chapter 57 Visit to a Cemetery on All Soul's Day

In General   SC 81–82; GIRM 346d, 379–385; BLS 110–114

Music   MCW 80, 83; LMT 22–26, 30–33

EUCHARIST OUTSIDE OF MASS

Sacramental communion received during Mass is a more complete participation in the eucharistic celebration. This truth stands out more clearly, by force of the sign value, when after the priest's communion, the faithful receive the Lord's body and blood from the same sacrifice . . . (HCWEOM 13; cf. GIRM 85).

The faithful should be instructed carefully that, even when they receive Communion outside Mass, they are closely united with the sacrifice that perpetuates the sacrifice of the cross. They are sharers in the sacred banquet which "through the communion of the body and blood of the Lord, the people of God share the benefits of the paschal sacrifice, renew the covenant with us made once for all by God in Christ's blood, and in faith and hope foreshadow and anticipate the eschatological banquet in the Father's kingdom, as they proclaim the death of the Lord until he comes" (HCWEOM 15; cf. EM 3).

In General

HCWEOM   Introduction 1–12, 13–15, 16, 17, 18, 19–22, 23–25

Communion Services

HCWEOM 26–41   The Long Rite with the Celebration of the Word
HCWEOM 42–53   The Short Rite with the Celebration of the Word
HCWEOM 113–188 Scripture texts

The use and frequency of this rite are regulated by the local ordinary. Contact your Office of Worship for further details.

Communion to the Sick/Viaticum

HCWEOM 54–78   Administration of Communion and Viaticum
                to the Sick by an Extraordinary Minister
                (Ordinary Rite 56–63; short rite 64–67)
PCS 197–211   Administration of Viaticum by a Priest or
                Deacon

Exposition of the Blessed Sacrament

HCWEOM 82–83   Explanation of Exposition of the Holy Eucharist
HCWEOM 84–92   Regulations for Exposition
HCWEOM 93–100   Exposition, Adoration, Benediction, Reposition
HCWEOM 101–108 Eucharistic Processions
HCWEOM 109–112 Eucharistic Congresses

HCWEOM 113–188   Scripture texts used during period of exposition; see also Lectionary #976–981; 167–169

Sunday Celebrations in the Absence of a Priest

This rite is not to be confused with chapter I of HCWEOM (13–53). SCAP is to be used on Sundays, led by a deacon or designated lay leader of prayer, and contains various options for celebration. It may only be used with the expressed permission of the local ordinary after careful assessment of the needs of the community, the availability of a priest, and possibility of a nearby Mass. The use of the rite is currently under review by the bishops of the United States.

BLESSINGS

The Church gives glory to God in all things and is particularly intent on showing forth his glory to those who have been or will be reborn through his grace. For them and with them, therefore, the Church in celebrating its blessings praises the Lord and implores divine grace at important moments in the life of its members . . . (BB:GI 12).

Function of Minister	SC 28–29; GIRM 91–94, 335, 352; CB 18–41
Laypersons	GIRM 107–109; LM 51–55; DMC 24; HLS 24, 29–38
Readers	BB Chapter 61; SC 29; GIRM 59, 101, 128–130, 194–198; LMI 14, 49–55; CB 30–32; GFT 103, 181
Instituted Readers	*Institution of Readers and Acolytes* (1972) #1–8
Extraordinary Ministers of Holy Communion	BB Chapter 63; HLS 24–26, 29–28; *Immensae Caritas;* Sacramentary Appendix V; GFT 72, 181
Altar Servers	BB Chapter 62
Sacristans	BB Chapter 62
Musicians	BB Chapter 62
Ushers	BB Chapter 62; GFT 44
Pastors	BB Appendix I
Catechists	BB Chapter Four, Section One
Pastoral Council	BB Chapter 64
Engaged Couple	BB Chapter One, Section Six
Married Couple	BB Chapter One, Section Three

FOR FURTHER READING

As I Have Done for You: A Pastoral Letter on Ministry by Roger Cardinal Mahoney and the Priests of the Archdiocese of Los Angeles (LTP)

Guide for Lay Preachers by Patricia Prachini (LTP)

Guide for Lectors by Aelrod Rosser (LTP)

Guide for Ministers of Communion by Vicki Tufano (English and Spanish) (LTP); Video Guide for Ministers of Communion (LTP)

Guide for Ushers and Greeters by Lawrence Mick (LTP) (English and Spanish)

WEEK OF PRAYER FOR CHRISTIAN UNITY

I do not pray for them alone. I pray also for those who will believe in me through their word, that all may be one as you, Father, are in me and I in you; I pray that they may be one in us, that the world may believe that you sent me (John 17: 20-21).

Since the 1920s, Christians have gathered, from January 18–25, to pray for the unity of all Christian Churches. These dates were chosen to coincide with the feast of the Chair of St. Peter (January 18 in the old calendar) and the feast of the Conversion of St. Paul (January 25).

It is highly advisable that planning meetings for these liturgical celebrations include representatives of the various Christian Churches. Even in the preparation of an ecumenical service, then, effective dialogue is produced. The service's structure, prayer, and readings should be familiar to all participants. For example, you may take an introductory rite from the *Book of Common Prayer,* a hymn from a Methodist hymnal, and a conclusion from the *Lutheran Book of Prayer* (cf. DAPNE #111).

Selected Resources

Book of Blessings   #553–573

Catholic Household Book of Blessings and Prayers #160

Directory for the Application of Principles and Norms on Ecumenism (1993), particularly Section IV

Graymoor Ecumenical Institute, 475 Riverside Drive, Room 1960, New York, N.Y., 10015-1999. 212-870-2330. www.atonementfriars.org

Lectionary   #867–871 For the Unity of Christians

Lutheran Book of Prayer; Book of Common Prayer; Various Hymnals

Sacramentary   Mass for the Unity of Christians (#13)
     Mass for the Spread of the Gospel (#14)
     Mass for Persecuted Christians (#15)

Unitatis Redintegratio, Decree on Ecumenism (Vatican II)

Ut Unum Sint, That All May be One, encyclical by John Paul II

MISCELLANEOUS OCCASIONS

Thanksgiving Day (USA)

Sacramentary	Proper Preface #84; Votive Mass for Thanksgiving Day
Lectionary	#943–947

Memorial Day (USA)

Sacramentary	Masses for the Dead
Lectionary	#1011–1016
Book of Blessings	#1734–1754 "Order for Visiting a Cemetery"

In Time of War or Civil Disturbance

Sacramentary	Mass in Time of War or Civil Disturbance Opening Prayers "For the President," "For the Congress"
Lectionary	#897–901 In Time of War or Civil Disturbance

For Peace and Justice

Sacramentary	Mass for Peace and Justice
Lectionary	#887–891

Respect Life Day (USA: January 22)

Sacramentary	Mass for Peace and Justice
Lectionary	Ps 139; #887–891
Respect Life Manual	1992 NCCB

Writing General Intercessions

SC 53–54; GIRM 36, 69–71, 138, 264; LMI 30–31; DMC 22, 29; MCW 74

Quinceara

In many Mexican American communities, when a young woman reaches the age of fifteen, she participates in a ceremony called *quince años.*

This is rooted in ancient Jewish traditions, in which a young woman was presented in the Temple. The ceremony ritualized her responsibilities to the community.

In the ancient Mayan communities, a young man became a warrior at age fifteen. So, too, a young woman was presented to the community because she possessed the ability to bear children—she was vital to the survival of the tribe because she could produce warriors.

In this century, women are still "introduced" to high society. The Quince Años ceremony, moreover, stresses a young woman's spiritual responsibilities in promoting the values of the Christian message.

Quinceara is not sacramental, but the sacraments of penance and Eucharist are sometimes integral to the celebration. The usual Order of Mass is followed. To it are added a renewal of baptismal promises, the dedication of the girl, and the blessing of the "gifts." These include a medal or crucifix (symbolizing religious expression of faith); a ring (to tie the young woman to her community and God); a crown (victory over challenges of her environment); and flowers (new life). Simplicity is advised to avoid the appearance of class distinctions.

For more information contact: Mexican American Cultural Center: A National Center for Pastoral Education and Language Studies, San Antonio, TX, 210-732-2156

DEVOTIONS

Popular devotions of the Christian people are to be highly endorsed, provided they accord with the laws and norms of the Church, above all when they are ordered by the Apostolic see. Devotions proper to particular churches also have a special dignity if they are undertaken by mandate of the bishops according to customs or books lawfully approved.

But these devotions should be so fashioned that they harmonize with the liturgical seasons, accord with the sacred liturgy, are in some way derived from it, and lead the people to it, since, in fact, the liturgy, by its very nature far surpasses any of them (SC 13).

Resources

Devotions and the Church Building	BLS 130–138
Devotions during Lent	PS 20
Handbook of Indulgence	Consult this small book for indulgence granted for the recitation of certain prayers or the performance of certain actions.

Marian Devotions

>
> *Marialis Cultis* by Pope Paul VI (February 2, 1974)
> May Crowning (by a bishop or priest) CB "Order for the Crowning of an Image of the BVM"
> Litany of Loreto
> Our Lady of Perpetual Help
> Guidelines for the Celebration of the Marian Year (USCCB)

Sacred Heart

>
> Cf. Sacramentary Votive Mass of Sacred Heart
> Cf. Lectionary #995–1000

Stations of the Cross	Various settings; copyright originally held by the Franciscans since they had been given care of the Holy Land in the sixteenth century. See new scriptural stations by John Paul II.

The Rosary

On October 16, 2002, Pope John Paul II issued an apostolic letter, *Rosarium Virginis Mariae*. In it, he reminds the bishops, clergy, and faithful of the universal Church that the rosary is a compendium of the Gospel message. While clearly Marian in character, "it is at its heart Christocentric" (RVM 1).

Prompted by the 120th anniversary of an encyclical of Leo XIII, Pope John Paul II declared October 2002 to October 2003 to be "The Year of the Rosary." He emphasized that the rosary should be prayed for the cause of peace and for the family. He noted, too, that it should be prayed in joyful remembrance of the fortieth anniversary of the opening of the Second Vatican Council (October 11, 1962).

The Pope offers us Mary as an incomparable model of contemplation who always kept her gaze on her Son. By meditating on mysteries of the rosary, then, we remember Christ with Mary, we learn Christ from Mary, we are conformed to Christ with Mary, we pray to Christ with Mary, and we proclaim Christ with Mary (RVM 5–17).

The Pope offered us a brief history of the rosary and lauded it as a compendium of the Gospel. With it, we can reflect on the incarnation and hidden life of Christ (the Joyful Mysteries), the sufferings of his Passion (the Sorrowful Mysteries), and the triumph of his Resurrection (the Glorious Mysteries). To that he added five new mysteries, a meditation on significant moments in Christ's public ministry—the Mysteries of Light or the Luminous Mysteries (RVM 21). All these mysteries lead us to meditate on the paschal mystery of Jesus Christ (RVM 24).

The Pope concludes with a chapter on improving the method for praying the rosary. This includes announcing the mystery, followed by the proclamation of a related Scripture passage, silent meditation, the Lord's Prayer, ten Hail Marys, the Gloria Patri, and a concluding prayer for the fruits of that particular mystery. He invites the Church to rediscover this simple, rich, and effective prayer and asked theologians and scholars to choose a variety of appropriate biblical texts and prayers.

The following page lists the mysteries of the rosary and offers suggestions for biblical texts that might accompany each mystery. You may choose others.

The Mysteries of the Rosary and Suggested Biblical Texts

Glorious Mysteries (Sundays of Easter Season and Ordinary Time; Wednesdays)

Resurrection	John 20:1-10
Ascension	Matthew 28:16-20
The Descent of the Holy Spirit	Acts 2:1-4
The Assumption of BVM	Revelation 11:19a; 12:1-6a, 10ab
The Coronation of BVM	Isaiah 9:1-6

Joyful Mysteries (Mondays and Saturdays, Sundays of Advent)

The Annunciation	Luke 1:26-38
The Visitation	Luke 1:39-45
The Nativity	Luke 2:1-7
The Presentation in the Temple	Luke 2:22-40
The Finding in the Temple	Luke 2:41-52

Sorrowful Mysteries (Tuesdays and Fridays, Sundays of Lent)

The Agony in the Garden	Matthew 26:36-46
The Crowning with Thorns	Mark 15:16-20
The Scourging at the Pillar	John 18:33–19:1
The Carrying of the Cross	Matthew 27:32-34
The Crucifixion	Mark 15:33-41

Mysteries of Light (Thursdays)

The Baptism of Jesus in the Jordan	Matthew 3:13-17
The Miracle at the Wedding in Cana	John 2:1-11
The Proclamation of the Gospel	Luke 1:1-4; 4:14-21
The Transfiguration	Matthew 17:1-9
The Institution of the Eucharist	1 Corinthians 11:23-26

Chapter IX

Conclusion

PREPARING TO PREPARE

And so you begin. You have reached for the correct books off the shelf, and you have even managed to mark the necessary pages with the ribbons. You've searched the hymnals for the perfect hymns and scoured the resources for the perfect setting for the psalm. You are all prepared to sit down around the table—the liturgist, the music director, the presider, the deacon, the homilist, the cantor, the artists, the sacristan, the lectors and other ministers, and even representatives of the assembly. You may even have copied the pertinent planning sheet found in the appendix of this book. But before you begin to simply "fill in the blanks," you must truly prepare to prepare.

First, begin with prayer. Ask for inspiration from the Holy Spirit. Reflect on the Word of God which the Church has selected or suggested for the day. Perhaps the Opening Prayer will help you to focus your thoughts and plans.

How will you shape the Introductory Rites? Will these rites enable the gathered assembly to form a community and to be attentive to the Word of God which will follow? Will a rite, such as an infant baptism, impact the Introductory Rites at this Mass? If this is not a Mass, what introductory rites does the rite provide?

What are the readings of the day? Who will proclaim them? Has the preacher or homilist had an opportunity to review them with a discussion group? Will another rite follow the homily? Who will compose the general intercessions or the Universal Prayer? How will these be related to the readings and to the needs of the Church and the world?

If this is a Mass, how does the Word lead us to the table of the Eucharist? How do we join our sacrifice to the sacrifice of Christ with and through the priest? How can the eucharistic prayer be better proclaimed (or sung)? What elements of the Communion rite might be better prepared and executed? Do the Communion procession and the song(s) reflect the fact that the fruit of the Eucharist is communion?

Do the brief concluding rites invite or charge the assembly to go forth and preach the kingdom?

How do the liturgical arts, including music, affect this celebration and the participation of the assembly?

Look at the celebration as a whole—are all its "parts" coordinated? Look at this celebration as a part of an entire liturgical season—is it in harmony with the celebrations that have gone before it and will come after it? Is every liturgy a celebration of our participation in the paschal mystery of Jesus Christ?

SO MUCH MORE TO LEARN

Over the course of these few pages, all I have provided is a fleeting glimpse into the beauty of the Church's liturgy. I have given you "Cliff Notes" on her liturgical books. I have summarized into inadequate paragraphs profound documents, written by committees of geniuses. I have encapsulated centuries of tradition into mere sentences. All of this can only give you a taste of the rich banquet that lies before you.

I invite you to study, in depth, the current rites and their ancient predecessors. Having accomplished that, you can be better suited to prepare liturgies for a twenty-first-century parish.

For in this era, we are no different than countless generations of Christians who have gone before us. We, too, are invited by God to encounter him in an act of worship. May we prepare our assemblies and ourselves to be worthy to stand in his presence and to give him due praise.

Appendix

Worksheets for
Preparing Parish Liturgies

MASS PREPARATION [SHORT FORM]

Date _____   Place _____

Solemnity/Feast/Memorial _____

Presider _____

INTRODUCTORY RITES

Hymn _____

Greeting _____

Sprinkling/Penitential   Invitation _____   Form _____

Glory to God   sung _____   recited _____   omitted _____

Opening Prayer   Sacramentary Page #_____   Option   A   B

LITURGY OF THE WORD

First Reading _____

Proclaimed by _____

Responsorial Psalm _____

Setting _____

Cantor/Psalmist _____

[Second Reading] _____

Proclaimed by _____

Gospel Acclamation/Verse _____

Setting _____

Gospel _____

Proclaimed by _____

Homily

[Other Rite]

Creed   sung _____   recited _____   omitted _____

General Intercessions

Minister _____

LITURGY OF THE EUCHARIST

Preparation of the Altar and the Gifts

Presentation Hymn _____

Gift Bearers _____

Prayer over the Gifts   Sacramentary Page #_____

Eucharistic Prayer
   Preface   Preface #_____

   Holy, holy, holy _____

   Eucharistic Prayer   I   II   III   IV   C1   C2   C3   R1   R2   MVNO

Lord's Prayer   sung _____   recited _____

Sign of Peace

Breaking of Bread

Setting: Lamb of God _____

Communion Hymn(s) _____

Meditation   Silence_____   Hymn of Thanksgiving _____

Prayer after Communion   Sacramentary Page #_____

CONCLUDING RITES

Announcements

Greeting

Blessing

Dismissal

[Closing Hymn] _____

LITURGICAL MINISTERS: EUCHARISTIC LITURGY

Date _____　Place _____

Solemnity/Feast/Memorial _____

Principal Celebrant_____

Concelebrants

_____　_____

_____　_____

_____　_____

_____　_____

Deacon _____

Master of Ceremonies _____

Reader #1 _____

Reader #2 _____

Proclaimer of Gospel (if deacon not present)_____

Homilist _____

Ministers of Holy Communion: Body of Christ [ordinary, then extraordinary]

_____　_____

_____　_____

_____　_____

Ministers of Holy Communion: Blood of Christ [priests, deacon(s), extraordinary]

_____　_____

_____　_____

_____　_____

Gift Bearers

_____　_____

_____　_____

Ministers of Hospitality

_____   _____

_____   _____

_____   _____

_____   _____

Thurifer _____

Cross Bearer_____

Candle Bearers

_____   _____

Music Director_____

Cantor_____

Choir(s)_____

Organist _____

Other Musicians _____

OTHER CONSIDERATIONS

Liturgy Coordinator _____

Coordinator of Environment _____

Producer of Worship Aids_____

Composer of Intercessions _____

Seating for Ministers _____

Seating for Persons with Disabilities_____

Interpreter for Deaf Community _____

Position of Gift Table _____

Microphones _____

Other Requisites _____

_____

_____

Ministers will vest in _____

Procession will form at _____

Order of Procession _____

_____

_____

_____

_____

Other Notes _____

_____

_____

_____

_____

Date _____   Solemnity/Feast/Memorial_____

Event _____   Place_____

Presider _____   Assistant_____

Cantor _____   Reader _____

LITURGY OF THE HOURS: MORNING PRAYER PLANNING SHEET

Date _____ Solemnity/Feast/Memorial _____

Event _____ Place_____

Presider _____ Assistant _____

Cantor _____ Reader _____

INVITATORY

Introductory Verse	Presider:	O Lord, ✠ open our lips.
	All:	And we shall proclaim your praise.
Doxology	All:	Glory to the Father, . . .

Antiphon

Psalm 29   or Psalm 100, 67, or 24. If one of these psalms occurs in the office, Psalm 95 is said in place of it. The psalm and its antiphon are omitted when the Invitatory precedes Morning Prayer.

—or when the hour does not begin with the Invitatory—

Introductory Verse   as above

Doxology   as above

Hymn _____

Based on Psalm 95 or other suitable hymn
which emphasizes praise, creation, morning, or light

PSALMODY

[Antiphon I]

Psalm _____ (sit)
On Friday, Psalm 51 or other penitential psalm

Setting _____

Psalm Prayer   (stand)

[Antiphon I]

OT Canticle _____

[Setting] _____

[Antiphon II]

Psalm _____   (sit)

Setting _____

Psalm Prayer   (stand)

[Antiphon II]

THE WORD OF GOD

Reading _____   (sit)

Silence

[Responsory]   *or suitable song*

GOSPEL CANTICLE

[Antiphon]

Canticle of Zachary/Benedictus   (stand)
> *(It is customary to sign yourself with the cross at the beginning of the Gospel Canticle. Incense may be used.)*

[Antiphon]

INTERCESSORY PRAYER

Petitions   *(which consecrate the day to God)*

Lord's Prayer

Collect

CONCLUDING RITE

Blessing

Sign of Peace

LITURGY OF THE HOURS: EVENING PRAYER PLANNING SHEET

Date _____ Solemnity/Feast/Memorial _____

Event _____ Place_____

Presider _____ Assistant _____

Cantor _____ Reader _____

INTRODUCTORY RITES

Introductory Verse	Presider:	God, come to my assistance.
	All:	Lord, make haste to help me.
Doxology	All:	Glory to the Father, . . .

Evening Hymn _____

OR

SERVICE OF THE LIGHT / LUCERNARIUM

Invitatory	Presider:	Light and peace in Jesus Christ our Lord.
	All:	Thanks be to God.

Hymn _____
        Phos Hilaron (O Radiant Light) or other suitable hymn

Thanksgiving for the Light

Presider:	Let us give thanks to God the Father always and for everything.
All:	In the name of our Lord Jesus Christ.
Presider:	. . . now and forever.
All:	Amen.

PSALMODY

[Antiphon II]

Psalm   (sit)
        Psalm of Day or Psalm 141   *(Incense may be offered.)*

Setting _____

Psalm Prayer   (stand)

[Antiphon I]

[Antiphon II]

Psalm _____ (sit)

Setting _____

Psalm Prayer   (stand)

[Antiphon II]

NT Canticle (see below)   (sit)

THE WORD OF GOD

Reading   (sit)

Silence

[Responsory]

[Other Rite]

GOSPEL CANTICLE   (stand)

[Antiphon]

Canticle of Mary (Magnificat)   Luke 2:29-32
> *It is customary to sign yourself with the cross at the beginning of the Gospel Canticle. Incense may be used to honor the altar, crucifix, and the assembly.*

[Antiphon]

INTERCESSORY PRAYER

Petitions

Lord's Prayer

Collect

CONCLUDING RITE

Blessing

Sign of Peace

> *Canticles*
> | | |
> |---|---|
> | Sunday—EP I | Phil 2:6-11 |
> | Sunday—EP II | Rev 19:1-17 |
> | Monday | Eph 1:3-10 |
> | Tuesday | Rev 4:11; 5:9, 10, 12 |
> | Wednesday | Col 1:12-20 |
> | Thursday | Rev 11:17-18; 12:10b-12a |
> | Friday | Rev 15:3-4 |

> *On Sunday, Evening Prayer I is said on the Vigil, Evening Prayer II on Sunday Evening. Except in Lent, the* Te Deum *is prayed in the Office of Readings.*

LITURGY OF THE HOURS: NIGHT PRAYER PLANNING SHEET

Date _____   Solemnity/Feast/Memorial _____

Event _____   Place_____

Presider _____   Assistant _____

Cantor _____   Reader _____

Introductory Verse	Presider: All:	God, come to my assistance. Lord, make haste to help me.
Doxology	All:	Glory to the Father, and to the Son, and to the Holy Spirit, as it was in the beginning is now and will be for ever. Amen.

Examination of Conscience

A brief examination of conscience may be made. In a communal rite, a penitential rite using the formulas of the Mass may be inserted here.

Hymn _____

PSALMODY

[Antiphon]

Psalm (see other side) _____

Setting_____

[Antiphon]

[Psalm] _____

[Antiphon]

THE WORD OF GOD

Reading _____

[Responsory]

GOSPEL CANTICLE

[Antiphon]   Protect us, Lord, as we stay awake; watch over us as we sleep,
that awake we may keep watch with Christ,
and asleep, rest in his peace.

Canticle of Simeon   *Nunc Dimittis* (Luke 2:29-32)

Setting _____

[Antiphon]

CONCLUDING RITE

Concluding Prayer _____

Blessing   Presider: May the all-powerful Lord grant us a restful night
                                    and a peaceful death.
                  All: Amen.

Hymn or Antiphon
in honor of the Blessed Virgin   *Regina Caeli* in the Easter Season

NIGHT PRAYER: PSALMS		
Day	**Psalm**	**Antiphon**
Sunday and Solemnities (after EP I)	4	Have mercy, Lord, and hear my prayer.
	134	In the silent hours of night, bless the Lord.
Sunday and Solemnities (after EP II)	91	Night holds no terror for me sleeping under God's wings.
Monday	86	O Lord, our God, unwearied is your love for us.
Tuesday	143	Do not hide your face from me; in you I put my trust.
Wednesday	31	Lord God, be my refuge and my strength.
	130	Out of the depths I cry to you, O Lord.
Thursday	16	In you, my God, my body will rest in hope.
Friday	88	Day and night, I cry to you, my God.

One may use Night Prayer from Sunday during the week.

MORNING PRAYER: THE FOUR-WEEK PSALTER				
WEEK I	**PSALM**	**CANTICLE**	**PSALM**	**READING**
SUNDAY	63:2-9	Dan 3:57-88, 56	149	Rev 7:10,12
MONDAY	5:2-10, 12-13	1 Chr 29:10-13	29	2 Thess 3:10b-13
TUESDAY	24	Tob 13:1-8	33	Rom 13:11b-13a
WEDNESDAY	36	Jdt 16:2-3, 13-15	47	Tob 4:15a, 16a, 18a, 19
THURSDAY	57	Jer 31:10-14	48	Isa 66:1-2
FRIDAY	51	Isa 45:15-25	100	Eph 4:29-32
SATURDAY	119:145-152	Exod 15:1-4, 8-13, 17-19	117	2 Pet 1:10-11
WEEK II				
SUNDAY	118	Dan 3:52-57	150	Ezek 36:25-27
MONDAY	42	Sir 36:1-5, 10-13	19	Jer 15:16
TUESDAY	43	Isa 38:10-14, 17-20	65	1 Thess 5:4-5
WEDNESDAY	77	1 Sam 2:1-10	97	Rom 8:35, 37
THURSDAY	80	Isa 12:1-6	81	Rom 14:17-19
FRIDAY	51	Hab 3:2-4, 13, 15-19	147:12-20	Eph 2:13-16
SATURDAY	92	Deut 32:1-12	8	Rom 12:14-16a
WEEK III				
SUNDAY	93	Dan 3:57-88, 56	148	Ezek 37:12b-14
MONDAY	84	Isa 2:2-5	96	Jas 2:12-13
TUESDAY	85	Isa 26:1-3, 7-9, 12	67	1 John 4:14-15
WEDNESDAY	86	Isa 33:13-16	98	Job 1:21; 2:10b
THURSDAY	87	Isa 40:10-17	99	1 Pet 4:10-11a
FRIDAY	51	Jer 14:17-21	100	2 Cor 12:9b-10
SATURDAY	119:145-152	Wis 9:1-6, 9-11	117	Phil 2:14-15
WEEK IV				
SUNDAY	118	Dan 3:52-57	150	2 Tim 2:8, 11-13
MONDAY	90	Isa 42:10-16	135	Jdt 8:25-27
TUESDAY	101	Dan 3:26, 27, 29, 34-41	144:1-10	Isa 55:1
WEDNESDAY	108	Isa 61:10–62:5	146	Deut 4:39-40a
THURSDAY	143:1-11	Isa 66:10-14a	147:1-11	Rom 8:18-21
FRIDAY	51	Tob 13:8-11, 13-15	147:12-20	Gal 2:19b-20
SATURDAY	92	Ezek 36:24-28	8	2 Pet 3:13-15a

EVENING PRAYER: THE FOUR-WEEK PSALTER				
WEEK I	**PSALM**	**PSALM**	**CANTICLE**	**READING**
SUNDAY I	141:1-9	142	Phil 2:6-11	2 Cor 1:3-4
SUNDAY II	110:1-5, 7	114	Rev 19:1-7	Rom 11:32-36
MONDAY	11	15	Eph 1:3-10	Col 1:9b-11
TUESDAY	20	21:2-8, 14	Rev 4:11; 5:9, 10, 12	1 John 3:1a, 2
WEDNESDAY	27	27	Col 1:12-20	Jas 1:22, 25
THURSDAY	30	32	Rev 11:17-18; 12:10b-12a	1 Pet 1:6-9
FRIDAY	41	46	Rev 15:3-4	Rom 15:1-13
WEEK II				
SUNDAY I	119:105-112	16	Phil 2:6-11	Col 1:2b-6a
SUNDAY II	110:1-5, 7	115	Rev 19:1-7	2 Thess 2:13-14
MONDAY	45	45	Eph 1:3-10	1 Thess 2:13
TUESDAY	49	49	Rev 4:11; 5:9, 10, 12	Rom 3:23-25a
WEDNESDAY	62	67	Col 1:12-20	1 Pet 5:5b-7
THURSDAY	72	72	Rev 11:17-18; 12:10b-12a	1 Pet 1:22-23
FRIDAY	116:1-9	121	Rev 15:3-4	1 Cor 2:7-10a
WEEK III				
SUNDAY I	113	116:10-19	Phil 2:6-11	Heb 13:20-21
SUNDAY II	110:1-5, 7	111	Rev 19:1-7	1 Pet 1:3-5
MONDAY	123	124	Eph 1:3-10	Jas 4:11-12
TUESDAY	125	131	Rev 4:11; 5:9, 10, 12	Rom 12:9-12
WEDNESDAY	126	127	Col 1:12-20	Eph 3:20-21
THURSDAY	132	132	Rev 11:17-18; 12:10b-12a	1 Pet 3:8-9
FRIDAY	135	135	Rev 15:3-4	Jas 1:2-4
WEEK IV				
SUNDAY I	122	130	Phil 2:6-11	2 Pet 1:19-21
SUNDAY II	110:1-5, 7	112	Rev 19:1-7	Heb 12:22-24
MONDAY	136	136	Eph 1:3-10	1 Thess 3:12-13
TUESDAY	137:1-6	138	Rev 4:11; 5:9, 10, 12	Col 3:16
WEDNESDAY	139:1-12	139:13-18, 23-24	Col 1:12-20	1 John 2:3-6
THURSDAY	144	144	Rev 11:17-18; 12:10b-12a	Col 1:23
FRIDAY	145	145	Rev 15:3-4	Rom 8:1-2

ORDER OF CHRISTIAN FUNERALS

Name of Deceased _____

Born into Life_____

Born into Eternal Life_____

Family Member(s) _____

Address _____   City _____

Phone(s) _____

Funeral Home Contact_____

VIGIL FOR THE DECEASED

Date of Vigil _____   Time_____

Location _____

Presider_____

Music Minister _____

FUNERAL MASS

Date of Funeral Mass _____   Time _____

Location _____

Presider_____

Music Minister _____

Placing of the Pall_____

Reader #1 _____

Reader #2 _____

General Intercessions _____

Gift Bearers _____

Eucharistic Ministers _____

Ministers of Hospitality _____

Pall Bearers _____

_____

Luncheon Information _____

VIGIL FOR THE DECEASED

INTRODUCTORY RITES

Greeting   A   B   C   D   Presider

Opening Song _____ Assembly

Invitation to Prayer _____ Presider

Opening Prayer   A   B   Presider

LITURGY OF THE WORD

Reading _____

Psalm _____

Gospel _____

Homily   Presider

PRAYER OF INTERCESSION

Litany   Presider & _____

Lord's Prayer   Invitation   A   B   C   Presider

Remarks _____

Concluding Prayer   A   B   Presider

CONCLUDING RITE

Blessing   Presider

FUNERAL MASS

INTRODUCTORY RITES

Greeting   A   B   C   D   Presider

Sprinkling with Holy Water   Presider

Placing of the Pall _____

Entrance Procession/Song _____ Assembly

Placing of Christian Symbols   yes   no

Opening Prayer   A   B   C   D   Presider

LITURGY OF THE WORD

First Reading _____

Responsorial Psalm _____

Second Reading _____

Gospel Acclamation _____

Gospel _____

Homily _____

General Intercessions _____

LITURGY OF THE EUCHARIST

Presentation of the Gifts _____

Preparation Song _____

Preface   Preface # _____

Sanctus   sung _____   recited _____   Assembly

Lord's Prayer   sung _____   recited _____   Assembly

Lamb of God   sung _____   recited _____   Assembly

Communion Song _____ Assembly

FINAL COMMENDATION

Words of Remembrance   yes   no _____

Invitation to Prayer   A   B   Presider

Silence

Signs of Farewell   yes   no _____

Song of Farewell _____   Assembly

Prayer of Commendation   A   B   Presider

Procession/Hymn_____   Assembly

Additional Comments _____

_____

_____

_____

FUNERAL LITURGY OUTSIDE MASS

INTRODUCTORY RITES

Greeting	A	B	C	D	Presider

Sprinkling with Holy Water

[Placing of the Pall]

Entrance Procession _____

[Placing of Christian Symbols] _____

Invitation to Prayer   Presider

Opening Prayer	A	B	C	D	Presider

LITURGY OF THE WORD

First Reading _____

Psalm _____

[Second Reading] _____

Gospel Acclamation/Verse _____

Gospel_____

Homily _____

General Intercessions _____

The Lord's Prayer   Assembly

[Holy Communion]

FINAL COMMENDATION

Invitation to Prayer	A	B	OCF #402	Presider

Silence   Assembly

[Signs of Farewell]   [Holy Water]   [Incense]   _____

Song of Farewell	OCF #201	OCF #403	Song	Assembly

Prayer of Commendation   A   B   Presider

PROCESSION TO PLACE OF COMMITTAL

Antiphon or Song   Psalm 25, 42, 93, 116, 118, 119   Assembly

RITE OF COMMITTAL

RITE OF COMMITTAL (used at the conclusion of a Funeral Mass)

Invitation						Presider
Scripture Verse	A	B	C	D	Other	Presider
Prayer over the Place of Committal	A	B	C	OCF #405		Presider
Committal	A	B	OCF #406			Presider
Intercessions	A	B	OCF #407			Minister
Lord's Prayer						Assembly
Concluding Prayer	A	B	CF #408			Presider

Prayer over the People
   Prayer   Presider
   Eternal rest . . .   Assembly
   Blessing   A   B

[Song] _____ Assembly

RITE OF COMMITTAL WITH FINAL COMMENDATION

Invitation	A	B				Presider
Scripture Verse	A	B	C	D	Other	Presider
Prayer over the Place of Committal	A	B	C	OCF #405		Presider
Invitation to Prayer	A	B	OCF #402			Presider
Silence						Assembly

[Signs of Farewell]   [holy water]   [incense]   _____

Song of Farewell   OCF #230   OCF #403   Other   Assembly

Prayer of Commendation   A   B

Committal   [or at conclusion of rite]

Prayer over the People
   Prayer   Presider
   Eternal rest . . .   Assembly
   Blessing   A   B

[Song]

THE SACRED TRIDUUM: HOLY THURSDAY
EVENING MASS OF THE LORD'S SUPPER

INTRODUCTORY RITES

Entrance Procession/Hymn _____

Greeting

Presentation of the Oils _____

_____

_____

Penitential Rite

Glory to God   Setting _____

Opening Prayer

LITURGY OF THE WORD

First Reading   Exodus 12:1-8, 11-14

    Lector _____

Responsorial Psalm   Psalm 116:12-13, 15-16, 17-18

    Psalmist _____

Second Reading   1 Corinthians 11:23-26

    Lector _____

Verse before the Gospel   John 13:34

Gospel   John 13:1-15

Homily

Washing of the Feet _____

_____

_____

_____

_____

_____

Acclamation(s) or Hymn _____

Profession of Faith   omitted _____

General Intercessions _____

LITURGY OF THE EUCHARIST

Presentation of the Gifts

   [oils] _____

   Gifts for the Poor _____

   Bread and Wine_____

   Presentation Hymn_____

Prayer over the Gifts

Eucharistic Prayer

   Preface   Preface #47

   Holy, holy, holy   Setting

   Eucharistic Prayer   Eucharistic Prayer I with embolisms

   Memorial Acclamation _____

   Great Amen _____

Communion Rite

   Lord's Prayer   sung _____   recited _____

   Sign of Peace

   Lamb of God _____

   Distribution of Communion

   Hymn(s) _____

   Prayer after Communion

Transfer of the Holy Eucharist

   Incensation

   Acclamation or Hymn _____

   Procession to Place of Reposition Blessed Sacrament

       Chapel _____   Other _____

[Stripping of the Altar]

THE SACRED TRIDUUM: GOOD FRIDAY
CELEBRATION OF THE LORD'S PASSION

Entrance of the Ministers   in silence

Prayer   A   B

LITURGY OF THE WORD

First Reading   Isaiah 52:13–53:12

    Lector _____

Responsorial Psalm   Psalm 31:2, 6, 12-13, 15-16, 17, 25

    Psalmist _____

Second Reading   Hebrews 4:14-16; 5:7-9

    Lector _____

Verse before the Gospel   Philemon 2:8-9

Gospel   John 18:1–19:42

Homily

Silence

General Intercessions

    Introduction

    Kneel/Silent Prayer

    Prayer

VENERATION OF THE CROSS

Form of Showing the Cross   Form One   Form Two

Invitation

Procession   to one cross

    Antiphon or Hymn _____

HOLY COMMUNION

[Covering of the Altar]

Ciborium to Altar

Lord's Prayer

Invitation to Communion

Distribution of Communion

  Hymn _____

Prayer after Communion

Prayer over the People

All depart in silence.

THE SACRED TRIDUUM: EASTER VIGIL

Lighting of the Fire

THE SERVICE OF LIGHT

Greeting

Blessing of the Fire

Lighting of the Paschal Candle

Procession

   Lighting of Assembly's Candles   *(those already baptized)*

Easter Proclamation/Exultet_____

LITURGY OF THE WORD

Introduction

Reading I	Genesis 1:1–22 [or 1:1, 26-31]
Responsorial Psalm	Psalm 104:1-2, 5-6, 10, 12, 13-14, 24, 35
	OR Psalm 33:4-5, 6-7, 12-13, 20-22
Prayer	
Reading II	Genesis 2:1-18 [or 2:1-2, 9, 10-13, 15-18]
Responsorial Psalm	Psalm 16:5, 8, 9-10, 11
Prayer	
Reading III	Exodus 14:15–15:1
Responsorial Psalm	Exodus 15:1-2, 3-4, 5-6, 17-18
Prayer	
Reading IV	Isaiah 54:5-14
Responsorial Psalm	Psalm 30:2, 4, 5-6, 11-12, 13
Prayer	
Reading V	Isaiah 55:1-11
Responsorial Psalm	Isaiah 12:2-3, 4, 5-6
Prayer	
Reading VI	Baruch 3:9-15, 32–44
Responsorial Psalm	Psalm 19:8, 9, 10, 11
Prayer	
Reading VII	Ezekiel 36:16-28
Responsorial Psalm	Psalm 42:3, 5; 43:3, 4
Prayer	

Gloria	(bells, lighting of church)
Prayer	
Epistle	Romans 6:3-11
Psalm/Alleluia	Psalm 118:1-2, 16, 17, 22-23
Gospel	Matthew 28:1-10, or Mark 16:1-8, or Luke 24:1-12
Homily	

LITURGY OF BAPTISM

Presentation of the Candidates for Baptism

Invitation to Prayer

Litany of the Saints   Setting _____

Blessing of the Water

Acclamation

Renunciation of Sin

Profession of Faith

Baptism

Clothing with a White Garment

Presentation of a Lighted Candle

Renewal of Baptismal Promises

Sprinkling with Baptismal Water

[Celebration of Reception into Full Communion]

   Invitation

   Profession of Faith

   Act of Reception

Celebration of Confirmation

   Invitation

   Laying on of Hands

   Anointing with Chrism

General Intercessions _____

LITURGY OF THE EUCHARIST

Preparation of the Gifts and the Altar

Presentation of the Gifts *(by the neophytes)*

[Presentation Hymn]

Prayer over the Gifts

Eucharistic Prayer

    Preface   Preface #21

    Holy, holy, holy _____

    Eucharistic Prayer   Eucharistic Prayer with embolism

    Memorial Acclamation

    Great Amen

Communion Rite

    Lord's Prayer

    Sign of Peace

    Lamb of God _____

    Invitation to Communion

    Distribution of Communion

    Silence or Hymn of Thanksgiving

    Prayer after Communion

CONCLUDING RITE

[Announcements]

Greeting

Solemn Blessing _____

Dismissal _____
                     Double Alleluia

[Closing Hymn] _____

RITE OF CONFIRMATION WITHIN MASS

Date_____   Parish _____

Presider _____   Pastor _____

INTRODUCTORY RITES

Hymn _____

Greeting _____

Sprinkling/Penitential_____

Glory to God   sung _____   omitted _____

Opening Prayer   Sacramentary Page #_____   Option   A   B

LITURGY OF THE WORD

First Reading _____

Proclaimed by _____

Responsorial Psalm _____

Setting_____

Cantor/Psalmist _____

[Second Reading] _____

Proclaimed by _____

Gospel Acclam/Verse _____

Setting_____

Gospel_____

Proclaimed by _____

SACRAMENT OF CONFIRMATION

Presentation of the Candidates_____

Homily or Instruction _____

Renewal of Baptismal Promises

The Laying on of Hands

The Anointing with Chrism

General Intercessions

Minister _____

LITURGY OF THE EUCHARIST

Preparation of the Altar and the Gifts

Presentation Hymn _____

Gift Bearers _____

Prayer over the Gifts   Sacramentary Page #_____

Preface   Preface #_____

Holy, holy, holy _____

Eucharistic Prayer   I   II   III   IV   C1   C2   C3   R1   R2   MVNO

Lord's Prayer   recited _____   sung _____

Sign of Peace

Breaking of Bread

Setting: Lamb of God _____

Communion Hymn(s) _____

Silence/Hymn _____

Prayer after Communion   Sacramentary Page #_____

CONCLUDING RITE

Announcements

Greeting

Blessing/Prayer over the People

Dismissal

Closing Hymn _____

Rite of Baptism for Children within Mass

Date _____   Time _____   Presider _____

Child _____

Parents _____

Godparents _____

Child _____

Parents _____

Godparents _____

Child _____

Parents _____

Godparents _____

INTRODUCTORY RITES

Hymn _____

Greeting

Reception of the Children

LITURGY OF THE WORD

First Reading _____

Psalm _____

Second Reading_____

Gospel Acclamation _____

Gospel_____

Homily _____

Intercessions _____

[Prayer of Exorcism and Anointing before Baptism]

CELEBRATION OF THE SACRAMENT

Blessing and Invocation of God over the Baptismal Water

Renunciation of Sin & Profession of Faith

Baptism

Explanatory Rites

    Anointing after Baptism

    Clothing with White Garment

    Presentation of a Lighted Candle

    [Ephphetha/Prayer over the Ears and Mouth]

LITURGY OF THE EUCHARIST

CONCLUDING RITES

Greeting

Blessing of the Mother(s)

Blessing of the Father(s)

Blessing of Assembly

Dismissal

[Closing Hymn] _____

RITE OF RECONCILIATION OF SEVERAL PENITENTS WITH INDIVIDUAL CONFESSION AND ABSOLUTION

INTRODUCTORY RITES

Opening Hymn _____

Greeting

Introduction

Opening Prayer _____

CELEBRATION OF THE WORD

Reading _____

Responsorial Psalm _____

[Second Reading] _____

Acclamation/Verse _____

Gospel _____

Homily

Examination of Conscience _____

RITE OF RECONCILIATION

General Confession of Sin

Litany of Repentance

   Response _____

Lord's Prayer

Individual Confession of Sin & Absolution

Proclamation of Praise for God's Mercy _____ Psalm, hymn, Magnificat, Other

Concluding Prayer of Thanksgiving _____

CONCLUDING RITE

Blessing _____

Dismissal _____

Closing Hymn _____

Rite I: Rite for Celebrating Marriage within Mass

ENTRANCE RITE

Rite of Welcome

Greeting of the Bride & Groom

OR

Entrance Procession   Order of Procession (see RM 20)

Hymn _____

Greeting

Penitential/Sprinkling Rite   Option _____

Glory to God   sung _____   omitted _____

Opening Prayer_____

LITURGY OF THE WORD

First Reading _____

Proclaimed by _____

Psalm _____

Sung by_____

Psalm Setting_____

Second Reading_____

Proclaimed by _____

Gospel Acclamation _____

Gospel_____

Homily

RITE OF MARRIAGE

Introduction

Questions

Consent [Vows]   Option   A   B

Blessing of Rings   Option   A   B   C

Exchange of Rings _____

General Intercessions

Profession of Faith   recited _____   omitted _____

LITURGY OF THE EUCHARIST

Preparation of the Altar and the Gifts

Presentation Hymn_____

Gift Bearers _____

Prayer over the Gifts

Preface   Proper Preface #_____

Holy, holy, holy _____

Eucharistic Prayer   I   II   III   IV

Lord's Prayer   recited _____   sung _____

Nuptial Blessing   Option   A   B   C

Sign of Peace

Breaking of Bread   Setting: Lamb of God _____

Communion Hymn(s) _____

Prayer after Communion

CONCLUDING RITE

[Announcements]

Greeting

Solemn Blessing

Dismissal

Closing Hymn_____

RITE II: RITE FOR CELEBRATING MARRIAGE OUTSIDE MASS

ENTRANCE RITE

Rite of Welcome

Greeting of the Bride & Groom

OR

Entrance Procession   Order of Procession (see RM #40)

Hymn _____

Greeting

[Opening Prayer]

LITURGY OF THE WORD

First Reading _____

Proclaimed by _____

Psalm _____

Sung by_____

Psalm Setting_____

Second Reading_____

Proclaimed by _____

Gospel Acclamation _____

Gospel_____

Homily

RITE OF MARRIAGE

Introduction

Questions

Consent [Vows]   Option   A   B

Blessing of Rings   Option _____

Exchange of Rings

General Intercessions and Nuptial Blessing

    Invitation

    Petitions

    Concluding Prayer   omitted _____

    Nuptial Blessing

If Communion is to be distributed, please see RM #54.

CONCLUSION OF THE CELEBRATION

Lord's Prayer

Blessing   Option _____

Rite III. Rite for Celebrating Marriage between a Catholic and an Unbaptized Person

RITE OF WELCOME

Greeting of the Bride & Groom [or begin with the Liturgy of the Word]

LITURGY OF THE WORD

First Reading _____

Proclaimed by _____

Psalm _____

Sung by_____

Psalm Setting_____

Second Reading_____

Proclaimed by _____

Gospel Acclamation _____

Gospel_____

Homily

RITE OF MARRIAGE

Introduction

Declaration of Intentions

Consent [Vows]   Option   A   B

Blessing of Rings   Option _____

Exchange of Rings

General Intercessions and Nuptial Blessing

   Invitatory

   Silence or Petitions

   Concluding Prayer   omitted _____

   Nuptial Blessing

CONCLUSION OF THE CELEBRATION

Lord's Prayer

Blessing   Option _____

Index